PRISM

LISTENING AND SPEAKING 3

Lewis Lansford
Robyn Brinks Lockwood

with
Christina Cavage
Angela Blackwell

CAMBRIDGE
UNIVERSITY PRESS

CAMBRIDGE
UNIVERSITY PRESS

University Printing House, Cambridge CB2 8BS, United Kingdom

One Liberty Plaza, 20th Floor, New York, NY 10006, USA

477 Williamstown Road, Port Melbourne, VIC 3207, Australia

314–321, 3rd Floor, Plot 3, Splendor Forum, Jasola District Centre, New Delhi – 110025, India

103 Penang Road, #05-06/07, Visioncrest Commercial, Singapore 238467

Cambridge University Press is part of the University of Cambridge.

It furthers the University's mission by disseminating knowledge in the pursuit of education, learning and research at the highest international levels of excellence.

www.cambridge.org
Information on this title: www.cambridge.org/9781009251280

© Cambridge University Press & Assessment 2022

First published 2017
Update published 2022

20 19 18 17 16 15 14 13 12 11 10 9 8 7 6 5 4 3 2 1

Printed in Mexico by Litográfica Ingramex, S.A. de C.V.

A catalogue record for this publication is available from the British Library

ISBN 978-1-009-25128-0 Student's Book with Digital Pack 3 Listening and Speaking
ISBN 978-1-316-62540-8 Teacher's Manual 3 Listening and Speaking

CONTENTS

Scope and Sequence — 4

How *Prism* Works — 8

What Makes *Prism* Special — 10

UNIT 1   Globalization — 14

UNIT 2   Education — 36

UNIT 3   Medicine — 58

UNIT 4   The Environment — 80

UNIT 5   Architecture — 102

UNIT 6   Energy — 124

UNIT 7   Art and Design — 146

UNIT 8   Aging — 168

Glossary of Key Vocabulary — 190

Video and Audio Scripts — 194

Credits — 223

Advisory Panel — 224

SCOPE AND SEQUENCE

UNIT	WATCH AND LISTEN	LISTENINGS	LISTENING SKILLS	PRONUNCIATION FOR LISTENING	
1 GLOBALIZATION _Academic Disciplines_ Cultural Studies / Sociology	NBA Fans in China	1: A radio program about the global food industry 2: A presentation about energy use in food production	**Key Skill** Activating prior knowledge **Additional Skills** Understanding key vocabulary Using your knowledge Listening for main ideas Listening for details Listening for opinion Understanding cause and effect Taking notes Synthesizing	Consonant clusters	
2 EDUCATION _Academic Disciplines_ Communications / Education	A Soybean-Powered Car	1: A meeting between a student and an academic advisor 2: A conversation between students about paths towards a medical profession	**Key Skills** Listening for advice and suggestions Making inferences **Additional Skills** Understanding key vocabulary Using your knowledge Listening for main ideas Listening for details Listening for opinion Taking notes Synthesizing	Certain and uncertain intonation	
3 MEDICINE _Academic Disciplines_ Health Sciences / Medicine	Corporate Wellness	1: A college seminar about pandemics 2: A debate about flu vaccines	**Key Skills** Identifying contrasting opinions Strengthening points in an argument **Additional Skills** Understanding key vocabulary Using your knowledge Listening for main ideas Listening for opinion Listening for attitude Listening for details Taking notes Synthesizing	Intonation in tag questions	
4 THE ENVIRONMENT _Academic Disciplines_ Ecology / Environmental Studies	Cloning Endangered Species	1: A lecture about habitat destruction 2: A talk about the decline of desert habitats	**Key Skills** Distinguishing main ideas from details Taking notes on main ideas and details **Additional Skills** Understanding key vocabulary Using your knowledge Listening for main ideas Listening for details Listening for opinion Listening for text organization Summarizing Taking notes Synthesizing	Sentence stress	

LANGUAGE DEVELOPMENT	CRITICAL THINKING	SPEAKING	ON CAMPUS
Modals of present and past probability Globalization and environment vocabulary	Understanding, analyzing, and using data in pie charts	*Speaking Skills* Presenting data Describing a pie chart Drawing conclusions from data *Speaking Task* Give a presentation using data from a pie chart on how we can ensure that workers in developing countries are paid fairly for the food we import.	*Presentation Skill* Involving the audience
Stating preferences with *would*	Prioritizing criteria Using priorities to evaluate options	*Speaking Skills* Giving an opinion and making suggestions Agreeing and disagreeing respectfully Compromising and finalizing a decision *Pronunciation* Certain and uncertain intonation *Speaking Task* Decide as a group which candidate should receive a scholarship.	*Communication Skill* Being an active listener
Health science vocabulary Conditionals: • Past unreal conditionals • Present and future unreal conditionals	Understanding background and motivation	*Speaking Skill* Using persuasive language *Speaking Task* Role-play a debate between representatives from an international aid organization and representatives from a drug company.	*Presentation Skill* Citing sources in a presentation
Multi-word prepositions The past perfect Verbs to describe environmental change	Organizing information in a presentation	*Speaking Skills* Giving background information Signposting *Speaking Task* Give a presentation about a change in the environment and discuss possible solutions.	*Study Skill* Time management

UNIT	WATCH AND LISTEN	LISTENINGS	LISTENING SKILLS	PRONUNCIATION FOR LISTENING	
5 ARCHITECTURE *Academic Disciplines* Architecture / Urban Planning	The Skyscraper	1: A conversation between two property developers 2: A housing development meeting	**Key Skills** Understanding figurative language Understanding strong and tentative suggestions **Additional Skills** Understanding key vocabulary Using your knowledge Listening for main ideas Listening for details Listening for attitude Taking notes Synthesizing	Emphasis in contrasting opinions	
6 ENERGY *Academic Disciplines* Engineering / Physics	Solar Panels at Home	1: A radio show about the island of El Hierro, Spain 2: A chaired meeting about saving energy in an office	**Key Skills** Understanding digressions Understanding persuasive techniques **Additional Skills** Understanding key vocabulary Using your knowledge Listening for main ideas Listening for details Listening for text organization Taking notes Synthesizing	Intonation related to emotion	
7 ART AND DESIGN *Academic Disciplines* Design / Fine Art	Jen Lewin's Light and Sound Installations	1: A radio report about graffiti 2: An informal debate about public art	**Key Skills** Inferring opinions Distinguishing fact from opinion **Additional Skills** Understanding key vocabulary Predicting content using visuals Using your knowledge Listening for main ideas Listening for details Listening for opinion Making inferences Taking notes Synthesizing	Stress in word families	
8 AGING *Academic Disciplines* Economics / Sociology	Baby Boomers' Retirement Style	1: A finance podcast 2: Two student presentations on aging in different countries	**Key Skill** Understanding specific observations and generalizations **Additional Skills** Understanding key vocabulary Using your knowledge Listening for main ideas Listening for details Taking notes Synthesizing	Consonant reductions and joined vowels	

LANGUAGE DEVELOPMENT	CRITICAL THINKING	SPEAKING	ON CAMPUS
Future forms: • *Will* and *be going to* for predictions and expectations Academic vocabulary for architecture and transformation	Analyzing and evaluating requirements for solutions	**Speaking Skills** Identifying problems and suggesting solutions: • Presenting a problem • Making polite suggestions • Responding to suggested solutions **Pronunciation** Emphasizing a word or idea to signal a problem **Speaking Task** Discuss a housing problem and possible solutions.	*Life Skill* Understanding college expectations
Connecting ideas between sentences: • Transition words and phrases The passive voice Academic vocabulary for networks and systems	Identifying, analyzing, and evaluating problems and solutions	**Speaking Skills** Keeping a discussion moving: • Asking for input, summarizing, and keeping a discussion moving • Dealing with interruptions and digressions **Pronunciation** Using a neutral tone of voice **Speaking Task** Participate in a discussion about an energy problem and suggest possible solutions.	*Communication Skill* Working in groups
Relative clauses: • Identifying and nonidentifying relative clauses	Debate statements and responses Taking notes for a debate Evaluating reasons Analyzing evidence	**Speaking Skills** Language for debates: • Expressing contrasting opinions • Restating somebody's point • Language for hedging **Pronunciation** Stress in hedging language **Speaking Task** Have an informal debate about whether or not public money should be spent on public art.	*Life Skill* Choosing a major
Verbs with infinitives or gerunds	Understanding, analyzing, and evaluating data from a line graph	**Speaking Skills** Referencing data in a presentation: • Explaining details and trends in a graph • Explaining causes and effects **Pronunciation** Contrastive stress in numbers and comparisons **Speaking Task** Give a presentation using graphical data on how aging has changed a country's population over time and the impact this is likely to have on its society in the future.	*Life Skill* The world of work

HOW *PRISM* WORKS

1 Video

Setting the context

Every unit begins with a video clip. Each video serves as a springboard for the unit and introduces the topic in an engaging way. The clips were carefully selected to pique students' interest and prepare them to explore the unit's topic in greater depth. As they work, students develop key skills in prediction, comprehension, and discussion.

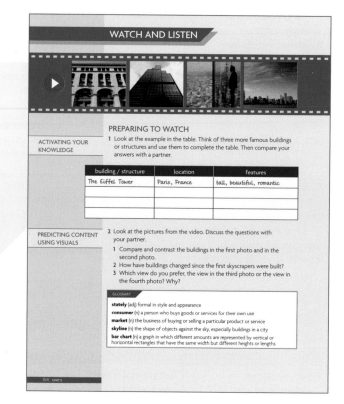

2 Listening

Receptive, language, and analytical skills

Students improve their listening abilities through a sequence of proven activities. They study key vocabulary to prepare them for each listening and to develop academic listening skills. Pronunciation for Listening exercises help students learn how to decode spoken English. Language Development sections teach grammar and vocabulary. A second listening leads into synthesis exercises that prepare students for college classrooms.

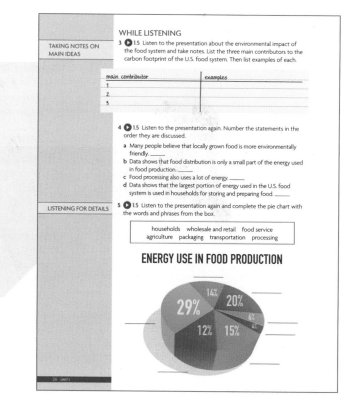

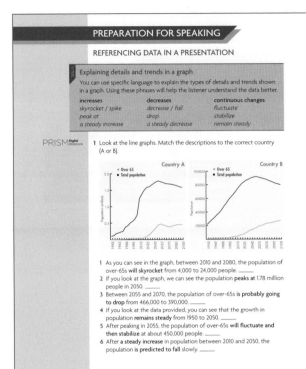

PREPARATION FOR SPEAKING

REFERENCING DATA IN A PRESENTATION

Explaining details and trends in a graph

You can use specific language to explain the types of details and trends shown in a graph. Using these phrases will help the listener understand the data better.

increases	decreases	continuous changes
skyrocket / spike	decrease / fall	fluctuate
peak at	drop	stabilize
a steady increase	a steady decrease	remain steady

1 Look at the line graphs. Match the descriptions to the correct country (A or B).

1 As you can see in the graph, between 2010 and 2080, the population of over-65s **will skyrocket** from 4,000 to 24,000 people. _____
2 If you look at the graph, we can see the population **peaks at** 1.78 million people in 2050. _____
3 Between 2055 and 2070, the population of over-65s **is probably going to drop** from 466,000 to 390,000. _____
4 If you look at the data provided, you can see that the growth in population **remains steady** from 1950 to 2050. _____
5 After peaking in 2055, the population of over-65s **will fluctuate and then stabilize** at about 450,000 people. _____
6 After **a steady increase** in population between 2010 and 2050, the population **is predicted to fall** slowly. _____

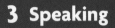

3 Speaking

Critical thinking and production

Multiple critical thinking activities begin this section, setting students up for exercises that focus on speaking skills, functional language, and pronunciation. All of these lead up to a structured speaking task, in which students apply the skills and language they have developed over the course of the entire unit.

ON CAMPUS

WORKING IN GROUPS

PREPARING TO LISTEN

1 Work in small groups. Discuss the questions.
1 Why do teachers often assign group projects to students?
2 What are the advantages of working in groups?
3 What can go wrong when people work in groups?

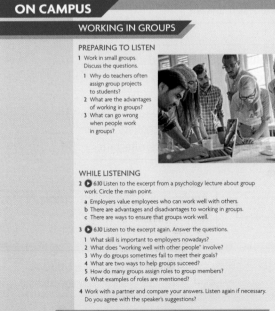

WHILE LISTENING

2 ▶ 6.10 Listen to the excerpt from a psychology lecture about group work. Circle the main point.
a Employers value employees who can work well with others.
b There are advantages and disadvantages to working in groups.
c There are ways to ensure that groups work well.

3 ▶ 6.10 Listen to the excerpt again. Answer the questions.
1 What skill is important to employers nowadays?
2 What does "working well with other people" involve?
3 Why do groups sometimes fail to meet their goals?
4 What are two ways to help groups succeed?
5 How many groups assign roles to group members?
6 What examples of roles are mentioned?

4 Work with a partner and compare your answers. Listen again if necessary. Do you agree with the speaker's suggestions?

Suggestions for working in groups
• Divide the work into stages
• Agree on a clear timeline
• Assign a role to each member of the group

---

4 On Campus

Skills for college life

This unique section teaches students valuable skills beyond academic listening and speaking. From asking questions in class to participating in a study group and from being an active listener to finding help, students learn how to navigate university life. The section begins with a context-setting listening, and moves directly into active practice of the skill.

WHAT MAKES *PRISM* SPECIAL: CRITICAL THINKING

Bloom's Taxonomy

In order to truly prepare for college coursework, students need to develop a full range of thinking skills. *Prism* teaches explicit critical thinking skills in every unit of every level. These skills adhere to the taxonomy developed by Benjamin Bloom. By working within the taxonomy, we are able to ensure that your students learn both lower-order and higher-order thinking skills.

Critical thinking exercises are accompanied by icons indicating where the activities fall in Bloom's Taxonomy.

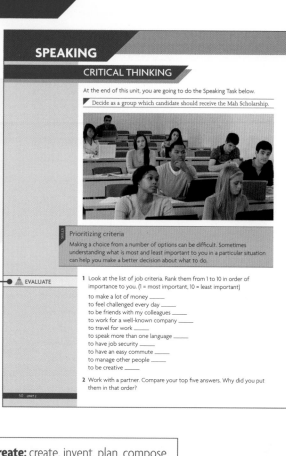

SPEAKING

CRITICAL THINKING

At the end of this unit, you are going to do the Speaking Task below.

Decide as a group which candidate should receive the Mah Scholarship.

Prioritizing criteria

Making a choice from a number of options can be difficult. Sometimes understanding what is most and least important to you in a particular situation can help you make a better decision about what to do.

⚖ EVALUATE

1 Look at the list of job criteria. Rank them from 1 to 10 in order of importance to you. (1 = most important, 10 = least important)

to make a lot of money _____
to feel challenged every day _____
to be friends with my colleagues _____
to work for a well-known company _____
to travel for work _____
to speak more than one language _____
to have job security _____
to have an easy commute _____
to manage other people _____
to be creative _____

2 Work with a partner. Compare your top five answers. Why did you put them in that order?

50 UNIT 2

Create: create, invent, plan, compose, construct, design, imagine

Evaluate: decide, rate, choose, recommend, justify, assess, prioritize

Analyze: explain, contrast, examine, identify, investigate, categorize

Apply: show, complete, use, classify, illustrate, solve

Understand: compare, discuss, restate, predict, translate, outline

Remember: name, describe, relate, find, list, write, tell

WHAT MAKES *PRISM* SPECIAL: CRITICAL THINKING

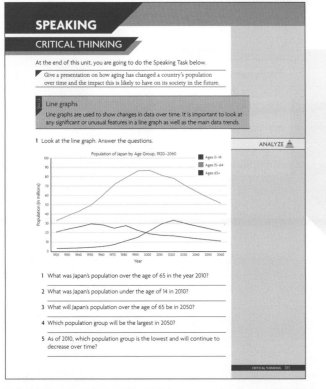

Higher-Order Thinking Skills

Create, **Evaluate**, and **Analyze** are critical skills for students in any college setting. Academic success depends on their abilities to derive knowledge from collected data, make educated judgments, and deliver insightful presentations. *Prism* helps students get there by creating activities such as categorizing information, comparing data, selecting the best solution to a problem, and developing arguments for a discussion or presentation.

Lower-Order Thinking Skills

Apply, **Understand**, and **Remember** provide the foundation upon which all thinking occurs. Students need to be able to recall information, comprehend it, and see its use in new contexts. *Prism* develops these skills through exercises such as taking notes, mining notes for specific data, demonstrating comprehension, and distilling information from charts.

WHAT MAKES *PRISM* SPECIAL: ON CAMPUS

More college skills
Students need more than traditional academic skills. *Prism* teaches important skills for being engaged and successful all around campus, from emailing professors to navigating study groups.

Professors
Students learn how to take good lecture notes and how to communicate with professors and academic advisors.

Beyond the classroom
Skills include how to utilize campus resources, where to go for help, how to choose classes, and more.

Active learning
Students practice participating in class, in online discussion boards, and in study groups.

Texts
Learners become proficient at taking notes and annotating textbooks as well as conducting research online and in the library.

WHAT MAKES *PRISM* SPECIAL: RESEARCH

LANGUAGE DEVELOPMENT

MULTI-WORD PREPOSITIONS

Multi-word prepositions are two- or three-word phrases that function like one-word prepositions, such as of, on, or by. Multi-word prepositions include:
- *two-word phrases (apart from, according to)*
- *three-word phrases (by means of, as well as)*

Like one-word prepositions, multi-word prepositions are followed by nouns, noun phrases, and gerunds. They show the relationship between two things. For example, in front of shows location.

1 Match the multi-word prepositions to the functions.

1 according to, based on	a making an exception
2 owing to, due to	b giving a source
3 apart from, except for	c giving another choice
4 together with, as well as	d including
5 rather than, instead of	e giving a reason

2 Circle the correct multi-word preposition to complete each sentence.

1 *Based on / Apart from* research that I carried out in Ethiopia, I can conclude that the destruction of deserts can be reversed.
2 Visitors rarely go to the research station *according to / due to* its extremely remote location.
3 *According to / Rather than* the latest *Economist Magazine*, share prices fell sharply last month.
4 The engineers decided to use solar power *owing to / instead of* conventional batteries.
5 The doctors used strong medication *as well as / except* for lots of liquid to help cure the patients.
6 The phone is assembled almost entirely by machines, *instead of / except for* the outer case.

3 Write your own sentences. Use a multi-word preposition with the function in parentheses.

1 (giving a source) _____
2 (giving a reason) _____
3 (giving another choice) _____
4 (including) _____
5 (making an exception) _____

LANGUAGE DEVELOPMENT 89

Vocabulary Research

Learning the right words

Students need to learn a wide range of general and academic vocabulary in order to be successful in college. *Prism* carefully selects the vocabulary that students study based on the General Service List, the Academic Word List, and the Cambridge English Corpus.

PRONUNCIATION FOR LISTENING

Sentence stress

In English, stressing different words can change the meaning or the focus of a sentence. Speakers often place more stress on key words, such as nouns, verbs, adjectives, and adverbs. Other times, they place more stress on words they want you to notice.

Conservationists want to protect the environment. (The speaker stresses *who* wants to protect the environment.)

Conservationists want to protect the environment. (The speaker stresses *what* conservationists want to do.)

8 ▶ 4.2 Listen to the sentence starters and underline the words the speaker stresses. The first two are done for you.

1 Sometimes, <u>natural forces</u> destroy animal habitats ...
2 <u>Sometimes</u>, natural forces destroy animal habitats ...
3 Humans have changed the Earth ...
4 Humans have changed the Earth ...
5 Humans have changed the Earth ...
6 Humans have changed the Earth ...

9 Match the sentence endings with the sentence starters in Exercise 8. Pay attention to word stress.

a ... but animals haven't changed it too much. __4__
b ... but most of the time they don't. _____
c ... but they haven't changed the sun. _____
d ... and you can't say that they haven't. _____
e ... rather than humans. _____
f ... and in some cases they've improved it. _____

10 Work with a partner. Practice saying the complete sentences.

DISCUSSION

11 Work with a partner. Discuss the questions.

1 How have people changed habitats in the country you live in?
2 Think of an environment you know. Which animals live there naturally? Do any animals live there that are originally from somewhere else?

88 UNIT 4

Pronunciation for Listening

Training your ears

This unique feature teaches learners to listen for specific features of spoken English that typically inhibit comprehension. Learners become primed to better understand detail and nuance while listening.

LEARNING OBJECTIVES

Listening skill	Activate prior knowledge
Pronunciation	Consonant clusters
Speaking skills	Present data; describe a pie chart; draw conclusions from data
Speaking Task	Give a presentation using data from a pie chart
On Campus	Involve the audience

uoi provarla

TOYO

ACTIVATE YOUR KNOWLEDGE

Work with a partner. Discuss the questions below.

1 Do you read any international magazines or watch foreign television shows or movies? Give examples of your favorites.

2 Do you like fashion or music from other countries? Why or why not?

3 What international restaurants or chains, such as McDonald's and Starbucks, are there in your city or country? What do they serve?

4 Do you buy any foods from other countries at the supermarket? If so, what foods do you buy?

WATCH AND LISTEN

PREPARING TO WATCH

ACTIVATING YOUR KNOWLEDGE

1 Work with a partner. Discuss the questions.

   1 Do you enjoy watching any sporting events that are played outside your country? Which one(s)?

   2 What are some sporting events that are popular around the world? Why do you think they are so popular?

PREDICTING CONTENT USING VISUALS

2 Look at the pictures from the video. Discuss the questions with your partner.

   1 What sport do you think the video is going to discuss?

   2 How do you think the people in the video feel about the sport? How do you know?

   3 Why do you think this sport is so popular in China?

GLOSSARY

NBA (n) the National Basketball Association; the men's professional basketball league in the United States and Canada

enthusiastic (adj) showing great interest or excitement

commissioner (n) an important official who leads an organization

banner (n) a long piece of cloth with words written on it

endorsement deal (n phr) a business arrangement between a company and a popular player in which the player represents the company in exchange for money

double-digit (adj) referring to the numbers from 10–99

haul in (phr v) to earn

WHILE WATCHING

3 ▶ Watch the video. Write *T* (true) or *F* (false) next to the statements. Correct the false statements.

UNDERSTANDING MAIN IDEAS

_____ 1 Since 1978 the NBA has organized nearly 150 international games.

_____ 2 The percentage of NBA games viewed by the Chinese population grew 40% in the previous year.

_____ 3 China is the second largest market for viewing basketball.

_____ 4 The NBA recognizes the opportunities that exist in China.

4 ▶ Read the main ideas. Watch the video again and write a supporting detail for each main idea.

UNDERSTANDING DETAILS

1 The commissioner was impressed with the number of fans that came to watch a practice.

_____

2 The players toured famous sights in China.

_____

3 The NBA anticipates double-digit revenue growth in China.

_____

5 Work with a partner and answer the questions.

MAKING INFERENCES

1 Why does the NBA appeal to the Chinese?

2 What are the advantages of bringing the NBA to China?

3 What can Chinese fans learn by watching an American sport?

4 What can the NBA players learn from visiting China?

DISCUSSION

6 Discuss the questions with your partner.

1 Have you attended an international sporting event? Describe it.

2 The reporter in the video says that *the language of sport proved universal*. What do you think he means?

3 Are there other aspects of American culture that are universal?

4 What other sports are popular outside the country where they began? Why did these sports become global?

LISTENING

LISTENING 1

PREPARING TO LISTEN

1 Read the sentences and write the correct form of the words in bold next to the definitions.

1 I **purchase** apples from a local market to help the environment.
2 Many educated **consumers** read the labels on their groceries.
3 Some farmers **produce** fruit and vegetables to sell locally.
4 The U.S. **imports** most bananas from other countries and then sells them in local supermarkets.
5 Scientists **investigate** the reasons climate change is getting worse.
6 According to the label on the spaghetti sauce, it is made **overseas**.
7 In cold climates, many types of fruit can be grown in **greenhouses**.

a _____ (v) to buy
b _____ (adv) in, from, or to countries that are across the sea
c _____ (n) a person who buys things for personal use
d _____ (v) to bring in from another country to sell or use
e _____ (n) a building used to grow plants that need constant warmth and protection
f _____ (v) to create something or bring it into existence
g _____ (v) to carefully examine something, especially to discover the truth about it

SKILLS

Activating prior knowledge

Thinking about what you already know about the topic before you listen can help you connect it to your own personal experiences or past studies. You can activate your prior knowledge by asking questions about the topic, looking at photos related to the topic, thinking about the title of the lecture or talk, or talking with a classmate about the topic.

You can ask questions such as:

- What do I already know about this topic?
- What experiences have I had that relate to this topic?
- What have I read or heard about this topic before?
- What do I think about this topic?

Activating prior knowledge will make it easier to understand key information when you listen the first time.

2 You are going to listen to a radio program called "The 11,000-Mile Fruit Salad." Before you listen, work with a partner. Think about the title and look at the photo on page 20. Choose the topics that you think will be included.

1 Supermarkets	5 Specialty food stores
2 Environmental pollution	6 American businesses in other countries
3 Job creation	7 Shipping food by air
4 International companies	8 Ways to make healthy food

WHILE LISTENING

3 ▶ 1.1 Listen to the interview between a customer and a reporter and check your answers to Exercise 2.

4 ▶ 1.1 Listen again and complete the student's notes. Then compare notes with a partner.

Name of program: The World Close-Up

Main topic: (1)_____

Customer interviewed: (2)_____

Customer is buying more (3)_____ and (4)_____ in order to

(5)_____

item	Pineapple	(6)_____	Kiwis	Mango	(7)_____
country or state	Guatemala	Ecuador	(8)_____	(9)_____	Mexico
miles	2,000	(10)_____	(11)_____	2,200	2,000

Must import food because (12)_____

Fruit and vegetables from hot countries must be grown in greenhouses, and this (13)_____

Total miles traveled: (14)_____

Problems with food traveling: long food supply chain and a huge carbon (15)_____

5 Read the statements. Write *T* (true) or *F* (false). Then correct the false statements.

_____ 1 Most of the food David is buying is imported.

_____

_____ 2 David usually tries to eat foods that are grown locally.

_____

_____ 3 The global food industry limits the types of fruit and vegetables people eat.

_____

_____ 4 You can be sure that locally grown food has not traveled very far.

_____

_____ 5 Locally grown food is always environmentally friendly.

_____

POST-LISTENING

6 ▶ 1.2 Listen to the excerpts from the radio program. Choose the statement that best matches the reporter's opinion about each excerpt.

1 a Cheap food can have hidden negative effects.
  b Cheap food costs less for consumers.
  c Cheap food is better for the environment.
2 a Shipping fruit by air is a good thing.
  b Shipping fruit by air is not environmentally friendly.
  c Shipping fruit by air is cheap and easy.
3 a Shipping fruit around the world might contribute to global warming.
  b The price of fruit at the supermarket is too high because of air travel.
  c If we don't eat enough locally grown fruit, we won't be healthy.

PRONUNCIATION FOR LISTENING

Consonant clusters

Mixtures of consonant sounds (consonant clusters) can cause problems with note taking. If you mishear the speaker, you might write the wrong word. Consonant clusters can be heard at the beginning of words (e.g., _grow_, _fly_, and _cross_) or at the end of words (e.g., _cost_, _passed_, and _find_).

7 ▶ 1.3 Listen to the consonant clusters in these sentences. Write the word the speaker says.

1 These agricultural products are already _____ abroad.
2 We grow many kinds of _____ on this plantation.
3 The police regularly _____ illegal imports.
4 The company _____ more clothes overseas last year.
5 The bananas are _____ so that they ripen together.
6 _____ the crops causes air pollution.
7 The products _____ through customs easily.
8 I want to know why these routes _____ more.

8 ▶ 1.4 Listen and complete the student's notes. Then read the notes and check that the words make sense with the context.

There hasn't been much (1)_____ from the government over the issue of imported agricultural crops. There are (2)_____ issues with this. (3)_____ , nearly a (4)_____ of all imported fruit cannot grow in our (5)_____ . Second, the (6)_____ should help our own farmers rather than foreign growers. Finally, we should not fall into the (7)_____ of not (8)_____ enough food. What (9)_____ happen if it didn't (10)_____ and we were left with a food shortage?

DISCUSSION

9 Work with a partner. Discuss the questions.

1 What fresh foods are often imported in your country?
2 Do you often buy imported fresh food? Why or why not?
3 Do you read the labels on the produce you buy at your supermarket? Where does it come from?
4 Do you think most people in your city or country buy food that has traveled long distances? Why or why not?

MODALS OF PRESENT AND PAST PROBABILITY

You can use modals to show how sure or unsure you are of something in the present or past. In the present, use a modal + base form of the verb. In the past, use a modal + *have* + past participle.

It **might be** a British company. (present)
It **might have been** a British company. (past)

Use *must* when you feel certain about something or when you think there is only one logical conclusion.

These avocados **must come** from Mexico. (present)
These avocados **must have come** from Mexico. (past)

Do not use contractions with *must*.

Alicia ~~**mustn't**~~ → **must not** be from Canada.

Use *can't* or *couldn't* when you are absolutely certain about something or when something is or was impossible or unlikely.

Can't have is relatively rare.
This sweater **can't be / couldn't be** from Japan. It's definitely from the United States. (present)
She **couldn't have bought** her car in the United States. (past)

When there isn't much evidence or when you are guessing, use *may, might, can,* or *could*.

The company **could be** British, but I'm not really sure. (present)
The store **might have imported** the bananas from Ecuador. (past)
Eun Sook **may not have worked** in the United States before. (past)

Only use contractions with *could* and *can*.

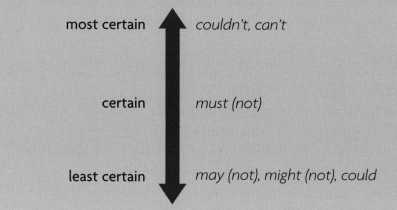

most certain	couldn't, can't
certain	must (not)
least certain	may (not), might (not), could

1 Circle the correct modal and verb form. Use the information in parentheses to help you.

1 Alana *couldn't have bought / may have bought* tickets to Ecuador last week. She asked me about ticket prices. (guessing)

2 Ahmed *must be / could be* from Oman. I saw his passport earlier. (the only logical conclusion)

3 I *might have lost / must have lost* my passport on the way home from work. It was in my pocket when I left work, and then it wasn't there when I got home. (the only logical conclusion)

4 Jin's new company *might send / must send* him to Dubai next week. They do a lot of international business, and he thinks a large meeting is happening in the next 30 days. (guessing)

5 My new smartphone *can't be / must be* from Tahiti. There isn't a big smartphone industry there. (impossible)

6 Luis *may have lived / must have lived* in South Korea for a while. He speaks fluent Korean, and I saw a Korean company on his résumé. (the only logical conclusion)

2 Complete the statements with modals of present and past probability. Use the given verbs and the clues in parentheses to help you. Sometimes more than one answer is possible.

1 Fruit and vegetables _____ (be) more expensive when they are grown locally. (present – logical conclusion)

2 Your smartphone _____ (be) made overseas and exported to be sold in other countries. (past – logical conclusion)

3 Your lunch _____ (contain) only food products that were produced in this country. (present – guess)

4 Fifty years ago, goods that were produced locally _____ (be) cheaper than goods that were produced overseas. (past – guess)

5 This movie _____ (be) based on an older British movie. The writer said it was American! (past – impossible)

GLOBALIZATION AND ENVIRONMENT VOCABULARY

3 Complete the text with the correct words and phrases from the box.

> carbon footprint   transportation   climate change
> processing   produce   supply chain
> carbon emissions   imported   purchasing

The Locavore Restaurant

simple, local food

A lot of us try to have the smallest possible (1)_____ , to reduce our impact on the environment, but almost all food (2)_____ , mostly by boat and airplane, produces (3)_____ that can harm the environment. Food (4)_____ , putting products into cans, for example, also uses a lot of energy. How can eating at a restaurant help with this? If you want to eat well without contributing to (5)_____ , try The Locavore. We serve delicious food that is less damaging to the environment. How? We keep our food (6)_____ as short as possible by (7)_____ our (8)_____ directly from farms within 25 miles of the restaurant and not buying a single ingredient (9)_____ from other countries. Our ingredients range from locally sourced fruit and vegetables to bread that we make on-site from wheat grown six miles away.

LISTING 2

PREPARING TO LISTEN

UNDERSTANDING
KEY VOCABULARY

PRISM **Digital** Workbook

1 Choose the best definition for the word or phrase in bold.

1 Colombia grows a lot of coffee beans. Coffee is one of the country's main **exports**.
   a products that a country sells to another country
   b products that a country buys from another country

2 Most supermarkets label fruit and vegetables so customers know the **source** of their produce.
   a the place where a product is made or created
   b the place where a product is used

3 The company uses salt when it **processes** salad dressing in order to keep it fresh during the long trip it takes to the supermarket shelves.
   a changes products back into their original materials
   b adds chemicals to a substance, especially food, in order to change it or make it last longer

4 Farmers use a variety of **transportation** methods, such as trucks, airplanes, and trains, when shipping their goods.
   a the condition of being alone
   b the movement of people or goods from one place to another

5 The new restaurant promised to use only **domestic** products when making its food. It will use only ingredients produced within six miles of the restaurant.
   a related to other countries
   b related to a person's own country

6 Joseph studied **agriculture** so he could manage his family's farm.
   a the practice or work of farming
   b the development of cities

7 There is an average of four people in each U.S. **household**.
   a a structure that supports a building
   b a group of people, often a family, who live together

2 You are going to listen to a presentation on energy use in food production. Before you listen, discuss the questions in pairs.

USING YOUR
KNOWLEDGE

1 What can farmers who live in cold climates do to raise plants that usually grow in hot countries?

2 Besides growing food, what other parts of the process use energy to get food to your table?

3 ▶ 1.5 Listen to the presentation about the environmental impact of the food system and take notes. List the three main contributors to the carbon footprint of the U.S. food system. Then list examples of each.

main contributor	examples
1	
2	
3	

4 ▶ 1.5 Listen to the presentation again. Number the statements in the order they are discussed.

a Many people believe that locally grown food is more environmentally friendly. _____

b Data shows that food distribution is only a small part of the energy used in food production. _____

c Food processing also uses a lot of energy. _____

d Data shows that the largest portion of energy used in the U.S. food system is used in households for storing and preparing food. _____

5 ▶ 1.5 Listen to the presentation again and complete the pie chart with the words and phrases from the box.

> households   wholesale and retail   food service
> agriculture   packaging   transportation   processing

ENERGY USE IN FOOD PRODUCTION

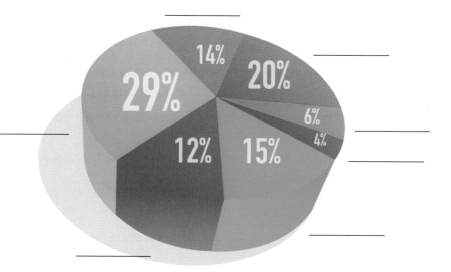

POST-LISTENING

6 Read the sentences from the presentation. Underline the cause of the action in each sentence.

1 It has been suggested that we should choose domestic foods over overseas exports because airplanes create pollution that causes environmental problems.

2 Experts argue that foods that are the least damaging to the environment are usually the ones grown locally. Consequently, some people believe that local foods are always more environmentally friendly ...

3 These greenhouses are heated, which therefore produces carbon dioxide.

7 Look at the sentences in Exercise 6 again. Circle the language that indicates the cause of the action in each sentence.

8 Complete the sentences with your own ideas. Then compare with a partner.

1 Due to improvements in food processing techniques,

_____ .

2 Food travels to supermarkets by airplane. As a result,

_____ .

3 Locally grown foods have a smaller carbon footprint. Consequently,

_____ .

4 Producing food packaging uses a lot of energy, which therefore

_____ .

DISCUSSION

9 Work with a partner. Describe a meal that you enjoy eating. Then discuss the questions.

1 Which countries do the ingredients come from?

2 Do you think it takes a lot of energy to produce the ingredients? Why or why not?

10 Work in small groups. Discuss the questions.

1 Look at the pie chart showing energy use in the U.S. food system in Exercise 5 on page 26. Think about food production in your country. In what ways would your country's pie chart be similar or different?

2 Use your notes from Listening 1 and Listening 2 to answer the following question. Would you change your food shopping habits based on what you learned about the environmental impact of the food system? If so, how?

SPEAKING

CRITICAL THINKING

At the end of this unit, you are going to do the Speaking Task below.

> Give a presentation on how we can ensure that workers in developing countries are paid fairly for the food we import.

SKILLS

Understanding a pie chart

Pie charts are used to show percentages. The sections of a pie chart represent portions of 100%, or the entire circle.

UNDERSTAND

1 Look at the pie chart. Answer the questions.

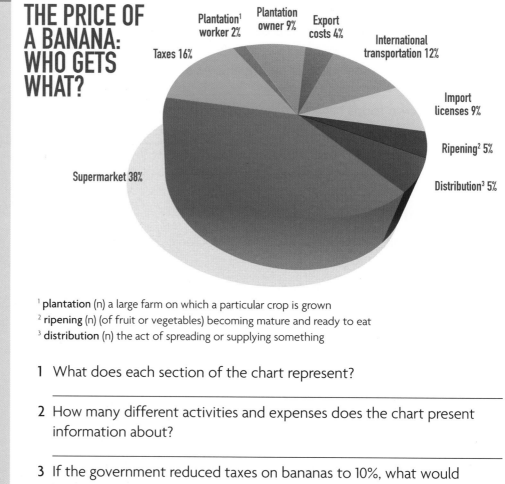

THE PRICE OF A BANANA: WHO GETS WHAT?

Plantation[1] worker 2%
Plantation owner 9%
Export costs 4%
International transportation 12%
Taxes 16%
Import licenses 9%
Ripening[2] 5%
Distribution[3] 5%
Supermarket 38%

[1] **plantation** (n) a large farm on which a particular crop is grown
[2] **ripening** (n) (of fruit or vegetables) becoming mature and ready to eat
[3] **distribution** (n) the act of spreading or supplying something

1 What does each section of the chart represent?

2 How many different activities and expenses does the chart present information about?

3 If the government reduced taxes on bananas to 10%, what would happen to the other percentages in the chart?

UNDERSTANDING DATA IN A PIE CHART

2 Look at the pie chart and answer the questions.

   1 What accounts for the biggest share of the price of bananas?
   2 What accounts for the smallest share?
   3 Which share is greater: *international transportation* or *distribution*?
   4 What share does *ripening* contribute to the price of bananas?
   5 What percentage of the total cost do *import licenses* represent?

ANALYZING AND USING DATA IN A PIE CHART

3 Does the pie chart support or oppose the following statements? Write *S* (support) or *O* (oppose).

   1 The cost of transporting bananas from the plantation to the supermarket accounts for the largest share of the price. _____
   2 Import licenses contribute nearly the same amount to the price of bananas as international transportation costs. _____
   3 The ripening process accounts for a much bigger share of the price of bananas than the growing process. _____
   4 Taxes contribute the smallest amount to the price of bananas. _____

4 Work with a partner and answer the questions.

   1 Why might supermarket costs contribute so much to the price of bananas?
   2 Why might the cost of growing bananas contribute so little?
   3 Why might plantation owners receive much more than workers?
   4 If governments reduced the cost of import licenses, what effect would it probably have on the supermarket section in the pie chart? Why?
   5 If plantation workers received twice as much money per banana, what effect would it probably have on the overall price of bananas? Why?

5 In this unit's Speaking Task, you are going to give a presentation agreeing or disagreeing with one of the statements below. Work with a partner and choose one of the statements.

   1 Food producers and exporters should be responsible for helping workers in developing countries get a fair deal.
   2 Governments in importing countries should take the lead in sharing their income from the food trade with workers in developing countries.
   3 Consumers should put pressure on supermarkets and distributors to do more for workers in developing countries.

6 Look at the pie chart in Exercise 1 and the statement you chose for your presentation in Exercise 5. Answer the questions.

1 Which segments of the chart relate to your statement?
2 What data evidence is there in the pie chart that supports your view?
3 What data evidence in the pie chart contradicts your view?

PREPARATION FOR SPEAKING

PRESENTING DATA

Charts present data in a way that makes it easy to understand. When giving a presentation, you can use charts to explain information that supports your point of view. You can make good use of the information by drawing general and specific conclusions from it, using figures such as fractions or percentages to describe it, and listing points and conclusions using sequential language.

PRISM Digital Workbook

1 Complete the introduction to the presentation. Use the words and phrases from the box.

a lot of discussion   consider   I'd like to talk about
many people believe   others have pointed out
look at   they say   would like to show

(1)_____ where your money goes when you buy a cup of coffee. There has been (2)_____ in the media recently about fair prices for the people in countries that grow crops like coffee. (3)_____ that it's not right that a cup of coffee can cost $4 or more, of which the farmers only get a few pennies. However, (4)_____ that the coffee beans are only one part of the cost of supplying a cup of coffee. (5)_____ that the other ingredients, such as milk and sugar, are also a big part of the cost of a cup of coffee. However, I (6)_____ that in a typical coffeehouse, the ingredients are only a small part of the overall cost. Let's (7)_____ some data. If you (8)_____ the information in this chart ...

2 ▶ 1.6 Listen and check your answers to Exercise 1.

DESCRIBING A PIE CHART

3 Look at the pie chart for the price of a cup of coffee in the United States. Complete the sentences with the phrases from the box.

> accounts for   a total of   each make up   a quarter of
> the largest part   three parts are related to   they make up

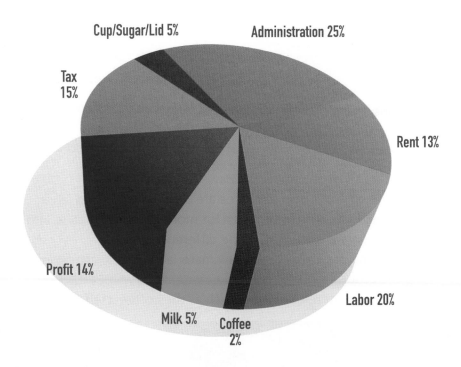

THE PRICE OF A CUP OF COFFEE IN THE U.S.

- Cup/Sugar/Lid 5%
- Administration 25%
- Tax 15%
- Rent 13%
- Profit 14%
- Labor 20%
- Milk 5%
- Coffee 2%

1 _____ of the cost is administration, at approximately 25%. That's _____ the cost per cup.

2 Labor _____ 20% of the cost.

3 Tax, profit, and rent _____ about 14% of the cost, or _____ 42% of the price of a cup of coffee.

4 _____ the product you take away – milk at over 5%; the cup, sugar, and lid at almost 5%; and the coffee itself at approximately 2%. Together, _____ just over 10% of the price you pay.

DRAWING CONCLUSIONS FROM DATA

4 ▶ 1.7 Listen to the next part of the presentation. Number the expressions in the order you hear them.

a as you can see ... _____
b This pie chart shows ... _____
c which you'll notice accounts for ... _____
d Finally, I'd like to draw your attention to ... _____
e Next ... _____
f First ... _____
g Second ... _____

5 Match the sentence halves.

1 You can see that in a typical cup of coffee, _____
2 This data shows that the raw ingredients only _____
3 This means that it may be possible _____
4 Looking at the chart, we can conclude _____
5 In summary, the data shows that the two biggest _____

a account for 12% of the price you pay.
b parts of the cost of a cup of coffee are administration and labor.
c that we could pay coffee farmers a lot more for coffee beans, and coffee drinkers wouldn't notice the difference.
d to increase the price we pay for raw materials without significantly raising the cost of a cup of coffee.
e the milk can cost three times as much as the coffee itself.

SPEAKING TASK

▶ Give a presentation on how we can ensure that workers in developing countries are paid fairly for the food we import.

PREPARE

1 Look back at the presentation statement you chose in Exercise 5 and your notes in Exercise 6 in Critical Thinking. Add any additional information that may help you.

2 Using the information in the pie chart in Critical Thinking, organize your points in the order you want to speak about them. Remember to put the most important points first and to support your points with data. Use language from the Preparation for Speaking section in your points.

3 Write notes and a conclusion to help organize your presentation.

4 Refer to the Task Checklist below as you prepare your presentation.

TASK CHECKLIST	✔
Set the context in the introduction.	
Describe the pie chart.	
Support your view with data.	
Draw a conclusion supported by the pie chart.	

PRESENT

5 Work with a partner. Take turns giving your presentation. Remember to use language from the Preparation for Speaking section to organize your talk and to present data.

ON CAMPUS

INVOLVING THE AUDIENCE

PREPARING TO LISTEN

1 You are going to hear part of a student presentation on food waste. Look at the two possible ways to begin the presentation. Which do you think is most effective? Why?

food waste in a landfill

A Today I'm going to talk about the problem of food waste. Consumers waste a lot of food every year. This is a problem because consumer-driven food waste in the U.S. costs approximately 165 billion dollars a year.

B First, let's see if you can answer this question: what percentage of food is thrown away in the United States every year? What do you think? Raise your hand if you think it's 10 percent ... 20? 30 percent?

2 Think of 2–3 other ways to keep the audience involved in a presentation.

WHILE LISTENING

3 ▶ 1.8 Listen to the presentation. Put the topics in order.

_____ global needs for food now and in the future
_____ how much food is wasted in the U.S. every year
_____ the effects on the environment of wasting food
_____ the financial cost of wasting food

SKILLS

Involving your audience

Use these strategies to involve your audience in your presentation.
- Begin with a story or a dramatic statement.
- Refer to audience experience.
- Rephrase statistics so that they can be understood easily.
- Ask questions.
- Ask the audience to react by standing up, raising hands, etc.

4 ▶ **1.9** Listen to the excerpts from the presentation. Work with a partner to identify the strategies the speaker uses in each excerpt.

PRACTICE

5 Match each sentence with a follow-up sentence.

1 First, let's see if you can answer this question. _____
2 Have you ever been to a farmer's market? _____
3 Raise your hands if you drank a cup of coffee this morning. _____
4 The salad you buy at the supermarket may be quite cheap. _____
5 You may be asking, how does this affect me? _____
6 You might think that the vegetables at the supermarket are local. _____

a But in fact, they may have traveled hundreds of miles to be packaged.
b But what is the environmental cost?
c Let me count ... That's almost everybody.
d Let's see a show of hands.
e Well, first of all, we are all directly affected by the cost of food.
f Where does most of our coffee come from?

REAL-WORLD APPLICATION

6 Work in pairs. Choose one of the graphs below. Decide what part of the information you would like to emphasize. Choose an aspect of the data that will be the most interesting to your audience.

7 Present the data in a way that involves your audience. Use some of the strategies from the skill box.

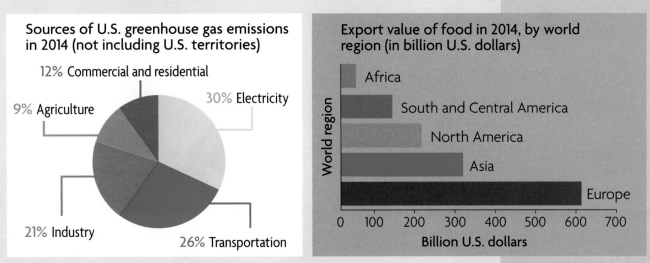

Sources of U.S. greenhouse gas emissions in 2014 (not including U.S. territories)

12% Commercial and residential
9% Agriculture
30% Electricity
21% Industry
26% Transportation

Source: United States Environmental Protection Agency

Export value of food in 2014, by world region (in billion U.S. dollars)

World region: Africa, South and Central America, North America, Asia, Europe

Billion U.S. dollars: 0 100 200 300 400 500 600 700

Source: WTO, Statista

LEARNING OBJECTIVES

Listening skills	Listen for advice and suggestions; make inferences
Pronunciation	Certain and uncertain intonation
Speaking skills	Give an opinion and make suggestions; agree and disagree respectfully; compromise and finalize a decision
Speaking Task	Make a group decision
On Campus	Be an active listener

ACTIVATE YOUR KNOWLEDGE

Work with a partner. Discuss the questions.

1 What careers require a lot of study? Which do not?

2 What subjects do you have to study to become ...
   • a teacher?
   • a doctor?
   • a lawyer?
   • a businessperson?

3 Would you like to work in a medical profession? Why or why not?

PREPARING TO WATCH

ACTIVATING YOUR KNOWLEDGE

1 Work with a partner. Discuss the questions.

1 What subjects are usually studied in high school?
2 What are some typical after-school activities?
3 Did you participate in any after-school activities? Which ones?

PREDICTING CONTENT USING VISUALS

2 Look at the pictures from the video. Discuss the questions with your partner.

1 Which of the cars do you prefer? Why?
2 How do people normally learn to work in a car factory? What high school or college subjects would be useful for this job?
3 Does the class in the fourth photo look like a typical high school class? Why or why not?

GLOSSARY

pique one's interest (phr v) to interest or excite; to make someone want to know more

hybrid (n) a type of car that uses fuel made from oil and another type of energy, usually electricity

soybean biodiesel (n phr) vehicle fuel that is made from a bean

rummage (v) to search for something by moving things around

mount (v) to fix an object onto something, such as a picture to the wall

dropout (n) a student who leaves school before finishing the course of instruction

stereotype (n) a fixed idea that people have about what a particular type of person is like, especially an idea that is wrong

---

WHILE WATCHING

3 ▶ Watch the video. Write *T* (true) or *F* (false) next to the statements. Correct the false statements.

_____ 1 A new sports economy car was the most popular car at the recent auto show.

_____ 2 The new sports economy car runs on biodiesel energy.

_____ 3 The car was designed and created by a large car manufacturer.

_____ 4 The auto shop class spent two years building the car.

_____ 5 Many of the students in the class had problems before joining the project.

4 ▶ Watch again. Complete the summary with the words from the box.

> attracted   difficulties   hybrid   an opportunity

In years past, big names like Ford, Toyota, and Ferrari (1)_____ a lot of attention at the auto show. The show in Philadelphia was different. The star of the show was a new (2)_____ car designed and made by a high school auto shop class. The students spent a year learning how to build a car, finding parts, and putting everything together. Prior to taking this auto shop course, many of the students had (3)_____ in school. Now, students like Cozy Harmon are earning good grades. Having (4)_____ like this is helping these students succeed in school.

5 Match the quotation with what can be inferred from it.

1 "Anything going zero to sixty in four seconds piques my interest." _____
2 "I was just getting by the skin of my teeth, C's and D's. I came here and now I'm a straight-A student." _____
3 "If you give kids that have been stereotyped as not being able to do anything an opportunity to do something great, they'll step up." _____

a The after-school project motivated him to do well.
b When presented with a challenge, students will work hard.
c Reaching high speeds quickly is important to the speaker.

DISCUSSION

6 Discuss the questions with a partner.

1 Would you like to have taken a class like this in school? Why?
2 What are the benefits of this type of school project?
3 Should this kind of class be required or voluntary for students? Why?

LISTENING

LISTENING 1

PREPARING TO LISTEN

USING YOUR
KNOWLEDGE

1 Check (✔) the statements that are true for you. Then discuss
them with a partner.

1 I have visited an academic advisor. ☐
2 I know what my major will be. ☐
3 I know a lot about the field I want to study. ☐
4 I know what I need to study for my future career. ☐
5 I have taken steps to prepare for my major. ☐

UNDERSTANDING
KEY VOCABULARY

2 Read the definitions. Complete the sentences with the correct form of
the words in bold.

> **academic** (adj) related to subjects that require thinking and studying
> **acquire** (v) to get or receive something
> **advisor** (n) someone whose job is to give advice about a subject
> **internship** (n) a short time spent training at a job in order to
> become qualified to do it
> **mechanical** (adj) related to machines
> **specialist** (n) someone with a lot of skill or experience in a subject
> **understanding** (n) knowledge about a subject
> **vocational** (adj) related to a particular type of work

1 John did his _____ at an advertising firm last semester. He learned a
   lot about how he could use his marketing degree after graduating.
2 To be a doctor, students need to take _____ courses such as
   biology and chemistry.
3 Students should attend a _____ program to become mechanics.
4 Taking English classes and practicing with others every day will help you
   _____ the language must faster than studying on your own.
5 I have a greater _____ of government since I took a course in
   political science.
6 Li visited her college _____ to help her choose her major.
7 People who study engineering generally have excellent _____ skills.
8 After she became a doctor, Carolina took additional courses to become
   a sports medicine _____ .

3 Work with a partner. Describe your study and career interests. Use the words from Exercise 2.

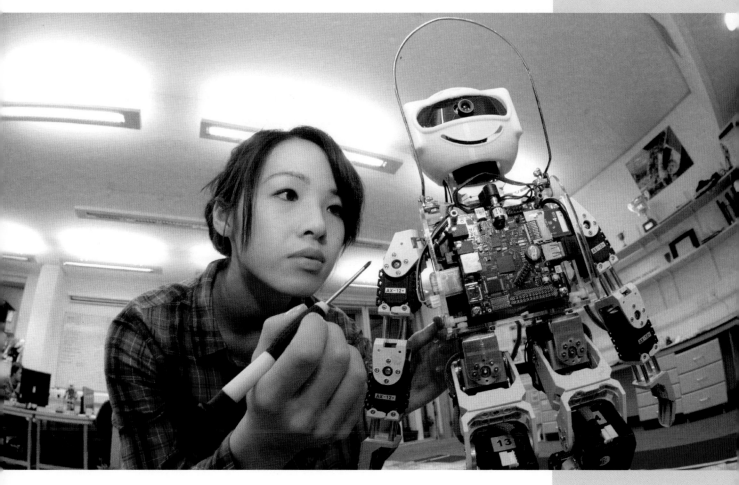

WHILE LISTENING

4 ▶ 2.1 Listen to the meeting between a student and an academic advisor. Then answer the questions.

LISTENING FOR MAIN IDEAS

1 What is Ada trying to make a decision about?

_____

2 What field is she interested in working in?

_____

3 What do Ada and the academic advisor decide she should do?

_____

Listening for advice and suggestions

When meeting with an academic advisor, it is important to listen for strong advice and suggestions. These are common phrases used to give strong advice and suggestions:

Strong Advice

You should (consider) ... / You ought to (consider) ... / I recommend ...

Suggestions

You might ... / You could ... / Have you thought about ... ? / Wouldn't you like/rather ... ? / I think ...

TAKING NOTES ON DETAILS

PRISM **Digital** Workbook

5 ▶ 2.1 Listen to the meeting again. Look at the notes that Ada took during the meeting with her academic advisor. Complete the notes with details that Ada missed.

1 Choose a career that will use _____ and _____ skills.
2 Consider _____ engineering.
3 Also consider aerospace _____ .
4 Find out more about engineering _____ .
5 Visit some _____ and engineering _____ .
6 Attend the _____ fair.
7 Talk to _____ at the fair about their _____ .
8 Contact a _____ engineering firm and arrange a _____ .

PRONUNCIATION FOR LISTENING

Certain and uncertain intonation

You can sometimes understand speakers' level of certainty by listening to their intonation. Intonation is the rise and fall of pitch in a person's voice. Rising intonation, with a questioning intonation, often indicates uncertainty. Falling intonation often indicates certainty.

▶ 2.2 Listen to these examples from Listening 1.

The world will always need engineers! ↘ (certain)

Maybe you should consider mechanical engineering, then. ↗ (uncertain)

I'd like to study something technical, that's for sure. ↘ (certain)

Maybe I could do an internship at an engineering company, and then study after I see how the internship goes. ↗ (uncertain)

6 ▶ 2.3 Listen to the statements and questions. Does the speaker sound certain or uncertain? Write *C* (certain) or *U* (uncertain).

1 __U__   5 _____
2 _____   6 _____
3 _____   7 _____
4 _____   8 _____

POST-LISTENING

7 Read the academic advisor's and Ada's statements. Do the words and phrases in bold show they are certain or uncertain about what they are saying? Write the bold words or phrases in the correct category in the table.

1 It would **definitely** be a way to use your math and physics skills.
2 I'd like to study something technical, that's **for sure**.
3 I **wonder** if I should try something more vocational.
4 Maybe you should **consider** mechanical engineering, then.
5 Okay, but I'm **not sure** if that would be for me.

certain	uncertain

DISCUSSION

8 Work with a partner. Discuss the questions.

1 Do you think the advisor gave Ada useful advice? Why or why not?
2 Do many people go to college in your country? Why or why not?
3 What kinds of jobs are popular with recent college graduates in your country?
4 In your country, what jobs do people do if they don't go to college?

STATING PREFERENCES WITH *WOULD*

Use *would rather* to express or ask questions about preferences.

I'd rather take a vocational course.

Would you **rather** start work right after graduation?

Use *would* (or *'d*) with verbs of preference, such as *like* and *prefer*.

I'd like to start working as soon as possible.

I'd prefer it if you studied a bit longer.

Would you **prefer** a short course to an academic degree?

Use *would rather* with the base form of a verb.

I **would rather** study engineering.

Use *would like* and *would prefer* with the infinitive form of the verb.

I **would like to study** engineering.

I **would prefer to study** engineering.

You can use *would prefer* and *prefer* with a noun, an infinitive, or a gerund.

Ada **would prefer an internship** at an engineering company.

Ada **prefers to work** at an engineering company.

Ada **prefers working** at an engineering company.

Use *or* in questions about preference to offer a choice between two things. Use the base form of the verb after *or*.

Would you like **to study at a university or attend a vocational program?**

Would you rather **study at a university or attend a vocational program?**

Would you prefer **to study at a university or attend a vocational program?**

1 Complete the sentences with the correct form of the verb.

   1 Let's talk about your courses for next semester. Would you rather *take / to take* art history or music appreciation?

   2 You need to consider where you would prefer to work. Would you like *work / to work* at a big company or a small one?

   3 She prefers *participate / participating* in team projects.

   4 Would you like *stay / to stay* home and study?

   5 He prefers *work / working* with his hands.

   6 Many parents would rather *see / to see* their children go to college than start work immediately after high school.

2 Rewrite each sentence using *would rather* or a verb of preference.

   1 Do you prefer to work for a lot of money or work for career satisfaction?

   _____

   2 I want to study for a master's degree.

   _____

   3 Do they want to apply to a university in Riyadh?

   _____

   4 He wants to consider studying medicine.

   _____

   5 Does she want to take a theoretical course?

   _____

   6 I don't want to start working right away.

   _____

PREPARING TO LISTEN

UNDERSTANDING KEY VOCABULARY

PRISM Digital Workbook

1 Read the definitions. Complete the text with the words in bold.

> **complex** (adj) involving a lot of different but related parts
> **manual** (adj) involving the use of the hands
> **medical** (adj) concerned with the treatment of disease and injury
> **physical** (adj) related to someone's body rather than the mind
> **practical** (adj) relating to experience, real situations, or actions rather than ideas or imagination
> **professional** (adj) connected with a job that needs special education or training
> **secure** (adj) dependable; not likely to change
> **technical** (adj) relating to the knowledge, machines, or methods used in science and industry

When I was younger, I wanted to be a doctor, but I don't think a (1)_____ job is for me. I'm considering going to a vocational school because it would give me training for a (2)_____ job such as an electrician or an information technology specialist. I would also not want to be a construction worker or firefighter, as those kinds of jobs require a lot of (3)_____ strength and energy. I enjoy (4)_____ work occasionally, like repairing electronics or other simple jobs around the house that I can do with my hands, but I'd like to have a (5)_____ career where I can use my education and training to do more (6)_____ things, like computer programming. I also want to have a (7)_____ job, so I'm not worried from one month to the next about having to find a new one. I'm very interested in physics, so if I don't go to a vocational school, I might consider studying something (8)_____ like engineering. My country is planning to build several new power plants in the next few years, and they'll need engineers.

2 You are going to listen to a conversation between Adam, a student who is interested in a career in medicine, and a medical student. Before you listen, read Adam's notes and discuss the questions in pairs.

Medical Jobs

Emergency Medical Technician (EMT)
Works independently in an ambulance. Helps people in emergency situations, assessing a patient's condition and performing emergency medical procedures before they get to the hospital. Must be confident. Requires excellent driving skills.

Emergency Room Nurse
Works in the emergency room of a hospital, dealing with patients as they arrive. Must have a high-level understanding of the human body and medicine and be able to assess patients quickly and correctly.

Which job do you think ...
- requires closer work with hospital staff?
- requires making decisions on your own?
- requires you to be sure of yourself and your abilities?
- requires more training?
- provides more excitement and adventure?
- requires more academic study?

WHILE LISTENING

3 ▶ 2.4 Listen to the conversation between Adam and the medical student. Write notes about the pros and cons for each job. Then compare your notes with a partner.

emergency medical technician (EMT)	emergency room nurse

4 ▶ 2.4 Listen to the conversation again. What is Adam's job preference?

_____

5 Check (✔) the speaker who expressed each opinion about the job. Then listen again and check your answers.

	medical student	Adam
1 That's a tough job. Exciting, but tough.	✔	
2 It seems like a great way to help people.		
3 You have to be very independent and confident.		
4 It would involve a lot more complex study.		
5 It would be great to actually work after so much study.		
6 It may not be the ideal program.		
7 I imagine the pay would be better.		
8 That's a great idea.		

POST-LISTENING

Making inferences

When listening, you can *make inferences* (draw conclusions) from clues rather than get information directly from someone's words. These clues can include tone (the pitch, or the way a person's voice goes up or down when speaking), facial expressions, and the emotion in someone's voice.

Consider these sentences: "You're late." and "You're here." What clues would tell you if the speaker was angry, concerned, surprised, or relieved?

MAKING INFERENCES

6 Work with a partner. Discuss the questions below. Think about tone and emotion.

1 What does the medical student really think Adam should do? How do you know?
2 What are the most important factors in a job for Adam? How do you know?

DISCUSSION

SYNTHESIZING

7 Work with a partner. Discuss the questions.

1 What areas of study do you think you already have the skills to do?
2 Would you like to become a specialist? If so, what kind?
3 What seems more interesting to you: a practical, vocational diploma or a more academic college degree? Why?
4 If you had to choose a career today, what would you choose? Why? What steps would you need to take to achieve that career goal?
5 Use your notes from Listening 1 and Listening 2 to answer the following questions. Where is the best place to get advice on education and careers? Would you choose an advisor, a graduate student, or a family member? Why?

SPEAKING

CRITICAL THINKING

At the end of this unit, you are going to do the Speaking Task below.

> Decide as a group which candidate should receive the Mah Scholarship.

Prioritizing criteria

Making a choice from a number of options can be difficult. Sometimes understanding what is most and least important to you in a particular situation can help you make a better decision about what to do.

▲ EVALUATE

1 Look at the list of job criteria. Rank them from 1 to 10 in order of importance to you. (1 = most important, 10 = least important)

to make a lot of money _____
to feel challenged every day _____
to be friends with my colleagues _____
to work for a well-known company _____
to travel for work _____
to speak more than one language _____
to have job security _____
to have an easy commute _____
to manage other people _____
to be creative _____

2 Work with a partner. Compare your top five answers. Why did you put them in that order?

Using priorities to evaluate options

Groups of people (project teams, managers, or groups of students) often need to decide how to use money or other resources. This involves discussing priorities, ranking criteria, and evaluating different options.

3 Work with a partner. Read the text and rank the criteria below for receiving the Mah Scholarship from 1 to 5. (1 = the most important, 5 = the least important) Discuss your reasons.

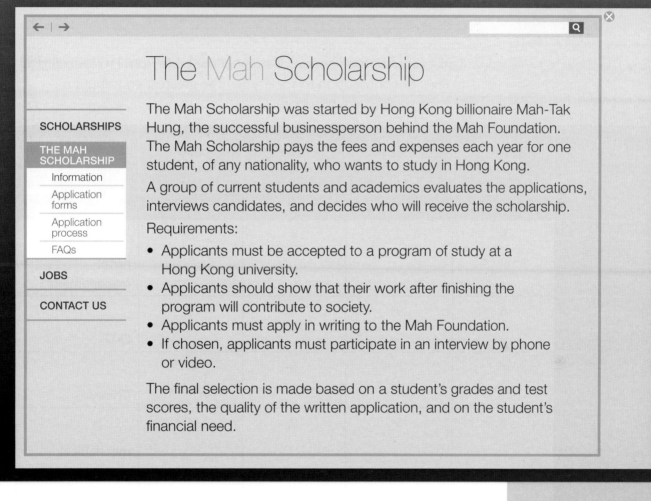

The Mah Scholarship

SCHOLARSHIPS

THE MAH SCHOLARSHIP
Information
Application forms
Application process
FAQs

JOBS

CONTACT US

The Mah Scholarship was started by Hong Kong billionaire Mah-Tak Hung, the successful businessperson behind the Mah Foundation. The Mah Scholarship pays the fees and expenses each year for one student, of any nationality, who wants to study in Hong Kong.

A group of current students and academics evaluates the applications, interviews candidates, and decides who will receive the scholarship.

Requirements:

- Applicants must be accepted to a program of study at a Hong Kong university.
- Applicants should show that their work after finishing the program will contribute to society.
- Applicants must apply in writing to the Mah Foundation.
- If chosen, applicants must participate in an interview by phone or video.

The final selection is made based on a student's grades and test scores, the quality of the written application, and on the student's financial need.

1 must be studying in a program that contributes to society _____
2 must include a good written application _____
3 must have a good interview _____
4 must have good grades and test scores _____
5 must be in financial need _____

4 Compare your answers with another pair. Did you rank the criteria in the same way? Why or why not?

5 Work in a small group. Discuss the questions and note your ideas. You will use this information for the Speaking Task at the end of this unit.

> The Mah Foundation committee has chosen five finalists for the scholarship. The table below summarizes its assessment of each applicant.

1 Which proposed course of study in the table will make the greatest contribution to society? Which will make the smallest contribution? Why?

_____

_____

2 Rank each proposed course of study in the table from 1 to 10 according to level of contribution to society. (1 = the greatest contribution, 10 = the smallest contribution)

name	interview score	written application score	grade point average	financial need	proposed course of study
Note: All scores are out of 10 possible points.					
Lee Jin-Sil	9	7	4	6	_____ hotel management
Adam Al Zamil	6	9	7	3	_____ EMT
José Lopez	4	7	6	8	_____ Chinese
Carolina Carrera	6	5	9	4	_____ mechanical engineering
Thomas Nguyen	7	4	9	6	_____ law

PREPARATION FOR SPEAKING

GIVING AN OPINION AND MAKING SUGGESTIONS

1 Match the sentence halves to make suggestions and give opinions. Which sentences make suggestions? Which give opinions?

1 I think the most important

2 I think

3 Why don't we

4 What if we say that

5 Have you considered

6 I feel it's important

a rank the proposed courses of study according to their contribution to society?

b to really focus on the applicants' potential contribution to society.

c looking at the applicant's family situation?

d the least important thing is the student's written application.

e factor is probably financial need.

f GPA, or grade point average, is the most important factor?

2 ▶ 2.5 Listen and check your answers.

AGREEING AND DISAGREEING RESPECTFULLY

SKILLS

In a discussion where speakers have different opinions, it is important to use formal language to disagree respectfully with what someone has said. You can do this in several ways.

- Using modal verbs before making a point:
  Yes, I can see that. It may not be the ideal program.

- Apologizing before disagreeing with someone's point:
  Sorry, but I have to disagree. I think being a doctor is a very practical job!

- Saying you recognize someone's point and then adding a *but* ... clause:
  Yes, but it seems like a great way to really help people when they need it.

3 Read someone's responses to another speaker. Is the person agreeing or disagreeing? Write *A* (agree) or *D* (disagree).

1 I can see what you're saying, but I have a different opinion. _____
2 I couldn't agree more. _____
3 I think that's right. _____
4 I'm not sure I share that point of view. _____
5 I'm sorry, but I have to disagree. _____
6 Yes, but have you considered other factors? _____
7 I'm with you on that point. _____

4 Work in pairs. Take turns reading your statements and responding. Use language from Exercise 3 and your own ideas.

Student A
1 Chinese will be the most important world language in the future.
2 Engineering is one of the best subjects you can study in college.
3 Lawyers are some of the most important people in society.

Student B
4 Everyone should be able to study at college for free.
5 Hotel management is an important college program.
6 It is more important to be able to speak English than to write it.

COMPROMISING AND FINALIZING A DECISION

5 Complete the sentences with the words from the box.

agreement   decision   point   right   that   understandable

1 I see. That's _____ .
2 OK, I see your _____ .
3 You might be _____ about that.
4 I think we can all agree with _____ .
5 Yes. We've made a _____ .
6 I think we've come to an _____ .

6 ▶ 2.6 Listen and check your answers.

PRONUNCIATION FOR SPEAKING

CERTAIN AND UNCERTAIN INTONATION

7 ▶ 2.6 Listen again. Do the sentences from Exercise 5 use certain or uncertain intonation? Write *C* (certain) or *U* (uncertain).

1 _____   3 _____   5 _____
2 _____   4 _____   6 _____

8 Work in pairs. Take turns saying the sentences in Exercise 5 with either certain or uncertain intonation. Can your partner tell whether you're being certain or uncertain?

SPEAKING TASK

> Decide as a group which candidate should receive the Mah Scholarship.

PREPARE

1 Look back at the criteria, the table, and your answers to Exercise 5 in Critical Thinking. Add any new ideas or information to your notes.

2 Refer to the Task Checklist below as you prepare for your discussion.

TASK CHECKLIST	✔
Give your opinion on criteria and priorities.	
Compromise with your group.	
Come to an agreement with your group.	
Respectfully disagree and make suggestions.	

DISCUSS

3 Get back into the group you worked with in Critical Thinking. Rank the candidates from the table in Critical Thinking, Exercise 5. Use the language in Preparation for Speaking to help you.

4 Based on your discussion from Exercise 3 and your work in Critical Thinking, decide who should receive the scholarship.

5 Choose one person from your group to present your choice for the scholarship to the class. Have him or her give reasons for the choice. Did everyone pick the same candidate? Who were the second- and third-place candidates?

ON CAMPUS

BEING AN ACTIVE LISTENER

PREPARING TO LISTEN

1 You are going to hear part of an orientation session for new international students at a university. Write *T* (true), *F* (false), or *NS* (not sure) next to each statement.

_____ 1 Most university classes carry three credit hours.
_____ 2 Students need to take 120 credit hours a year.
_____ 3 Most students take 12–15 credit hours a semester.
_____ 4 A three-credit class meets for about six hours a week.
_____ 5 You can sometimes get credit for classes that you have taken before you start college.
_____ 6 Most teachers use a letter grading system.
_____ 7 To pass a class, you need to get at least a B.
_____ 8 Your grade point average (GPA) is your average grade over time.

WHILE LISTENING

2 ▶ 2.7 Listen and check your answers to Exercise 1. Compare your answers with a partner.

3 ▶ 2.7 Listen again. Complete the questions and phrases that the students use.

1 I'm sorry, can you please _____ ?
2 May I _____ ?
3 Is that _____ ?
4 So in _____ ?
5 Can you _____ ?
6 Could I _____ ?
7 Can you _____ ?

SKILLS

Being an active listener

- Check that you understand what is being said.
- Ask speakers to repeat, clarify, or give an example.
- Restate the information in your own words to check your understanding.
- Ask permission before you ask a question, and thank the speaker for the reply.

PRACTICE

4 Match the phrases with their functions.

1 Can you give us an example? _____
2 Could you please say that again? _____
3 May I ask a question? _____
4 So in other words, ... _____
5 Somebody told me that ... Is that correct? _____
6 What's the difference between ... ? _____

a asking for an example
b asking for confirmation
c asking a speaker to repeat
d asking for an explanation
e asking permission to ask a question
f restating to check understanding

5 Complete the conversation with one of the phrases above. Then practice the conversation with a partner.

Student: Somebody told me it's possible to have a double major.
(1)_____ ?

Instructor: Yes, you can have a double major. About one-third of our students do that.

Student: (2)_____ ?

Instructor: Well, let's say your major is biology. But you also take a lot of music classes. Your music classes could count towards a major in music.

Student: (3)_____ , you study two major subjects.

Instructor: That's right.

Student: (4)_____ a major and a minor?

Instructor: In both cases you are concentrating on one subject, but a minor involves fewer classes.

REAL-WORLD APPLICATION

6 Look at the words and phrases in the box. They are all commonly used in schools and universities. Circle the expressions that you understand. Use a dictionary if necessary.

> a semester   a required class   an elective class   a prerequisite class
> office hours   a transcript   a syllabus   a due date

7 Work in groups. Have each student choose 1–3 words to explain. Take turns explaining each word. During the explanations, ask the speaker for repetition and clarification.

Listening skills	Identify contrasting opinions; strengthen points in an argument
Pronunciation	Intonation in tag questions
Speaking skill	Use persuasive language
Speaking Task	Role-play a debate
On Campus	Cite sources in a presentation

ACTIVATE YOUR KNOWLEDGE

Work with a partner. Discuss the questions below.

1 What are some common illnesses or medical problems? How are they treated?

2 How do illnesses usually spread from person to person?

3 The baby in the photo is being given a vaccine to avoid getting a disease. What diseases have vaccines? What diseases do not?

4 Do you think vaccines are a good idea? Why or why not?

WATCH AND LISTEN

PREPARING TO WATCH

ACTIVATING YOUR KNOWLEDGE

1 Work with a partner. Discuss the questions.

   1 What are the most common medical problems today? How are they usually treated?

   2 What can employers do to help their employees prevent these medical problems?

   3 What are the benefits of company health programs?

PREDICTING CONTENT USING VISUALS

2 Look at the pictures from the video. Discuss the questions with your partner.

   1 Should employees exercise at work?

   2 What tools or devices do you see? What are they used for?

   3 Where do you think the woman in the last picture is?

GLOSSARY

up-and-down battle (n phr) a fight that repeatedly moves in one direction and then in the opposite direction

spark (n) a small idea or event that causes something bigger to start

motivate (v) to make someone enthusiastic about doing something

productivity (n) the rate at which a person, company, or country does useful work

corporate wellness program (n) information and activities provided by a company to improve the health of its employees

pedometer (n) a device that measures how many steps a person walks

cardio (n) physical exercise that increases your heart rate

WHILE WATCHING

3 ▶ Watch the video. Write *T* (true) or *F* (false) next to the statements. Correct the false statements.

UNDERSTANDING
MAIN IDEAS

_____ 1 Making extra money was motivation for Donna to lose weight.

_____ 2 The program only benefits employees.

_____ 3 Employees in the program are sick more often and are more productive.

_____ 4 People in the program receive a tool to track their steps.

_____ 5 Corporate wellness programs often have on-site gyms where employees can take a cardio class after their work day.

4 ▶ Watch again. Complete the notes.

UNDERSTANDING
DETAILS

Motivation for Donna to get healthy: (1)_____

_____

How much her company pays employees to improve health:

(2)_____

Four benefits to the company: (3)_____

_____

Number of steps Donna has taken: (4)_____

Type of food in cafeteria: (5)_____

5 Work with a partner and discuss the questions.

MAKING INFERENCES

1 What other benefits do you think Donna Sharples has received from the changes she made?

2 What changes do you think Donna's company had to make in order to offer a corporate wellness program?

3 What advances in technology have helped people become more aware of their health?

DISCUSSION

6 Discuss the questions with your partner.

1 Do you think it is important for companies to make their employees' health a priority? Why or why not?

2 How else could companies motivate their employees to be healthy?

3 What other tools or devices exist today that help people track their health?

LISTENING

LISTENING 1

PREPARING TO LISTEN

UNDERSTANDING
KEY VOCABULARY

1 You are going to listen to a seminar about pandemics. Before you listen, read the sentences and write the words in bold next to the definitions.

1 The doctor **contracted** the flu when he was treating patients with the same disease.
2 Cost is an important **factor** in deciding whether to pay for a vaccine.
3 A mosquito bit Lu last summer. Lu became **infected** with dengue when the mosquito bit him.
4 Doctors state that most colds **occur** after someone touches a surface that has the cold virus on it.
5 The Ebola **outbreak** was sudden and spread very quickly to thousands of people. Now there is a vaccine in development.
6 **Prevention** of the flu focuses on washing your hands often and getting a flu shot every year.
7 It takes a long time to **recover** from surgery. My uncle was tired and felt some pain for several weeks before he felt normal again.
8 Juan is receiving **treatment** for his back pain. He says it is helping because his back does not hurt as much as before.

a _____ (v) to happen
b _____ (v) to become completely well again after an illness or injury
c _____ (v) to catch or become ill with a disease
d _____ (adj) having a disease as a result of the introduction of organisms such as bacteria or viruses to the body
e _____ (n) the act of stopping something from happening
f _____ (n) a sudden appearance of something, especially of a disease or something else dangerous or unpleasant
g _____ (n) something that you do to try to cure an illness or injury, especially something suggested by a doctor
h _____ (n) a fact or situation that influences the result of something

2 Read the text and look at the map. Then answer the questions below.

A pandemic is when a contagious disease spreads through the human population in a large region. This could be across multiple countries, or even the whole world. Throughout history there have been a number of pandemics, such as flu and cholera. A disease must be infectious (passed directly from person to person) for it to be considered a pandemic.

Risk of influenza pandemics across the globe

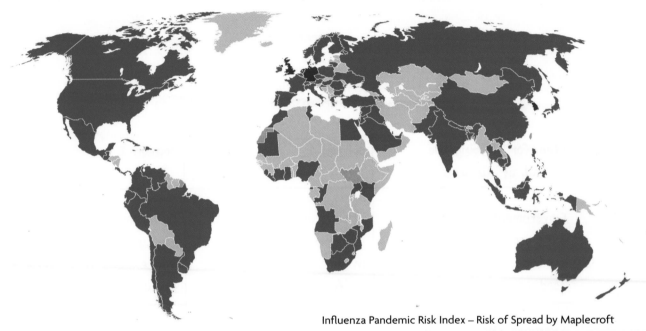

Influenza Pandemic Risk Index – Risk of Spread by Maplecroft

1 What are the factors in the spread of a disease? How can it be prevented from spreading?

2 What would make a country at high risk for a pandemic? Think about:

- size of population
- density of population
- size of cities
- number of international airports
- borders with other countries
- number of hospitals

3 Look at the map. Which color do you think represents countries at high risk for pandemics? Which color represents countries at low risk? What is the risk level in your country?

WHILE LISTENING

3 ▶ 3.1 Listen to the seminar and check your answers to Exercise 2.

4 ▶ 3.1 Listen to the seminar again. Take notes as you listen and focus on these questions. What might cause a pandemic? What factors make a country at high risk for a pandemic?

5 Compare your notes with a partner and write any missing information.

SKILLS

Identifying contrasting opinions

In a discussion, a group considers and explores different ideas. Key phrases such as *In my opinion …* and *As far as I'm concerned …* indicate opinions and can help you separate facts from what somebody thinks. Most phrases are used at the beginning of a sentence to let the listener know that it is the speaker's opinion.

As far as I'm concerned, all parents should vaccinate their children.

Other phrases used at the beginning of a sentence include:

I think …	As I see it …	To me …
I believe …	It seems to me …	From my perspective …

PRISM Digital Workbook

6 ▶ 3.1 Listen again and complete the student's notes with the different opinions. Then compare your answers with a partner.

idea for stopping the spread of disease	opinion 1	opinion 2
Governments must make sure populations are in good health and live in good conditions.	There's a limit to what governments can do in times of economic difficulty.	Governments don't always have the power to say exactly how everyone should live.
Everyone should be forced to get vaccines.	(1)	(2)
People with diseases shouldn't be allowed into the country.	(3)	(4)
All flights from countries with a pandemic should be stopped.	(5)	(6)

POST-LISTENING

7 ▶ 3.2 Listen to the tag questions from the listening. What does the speaker mean? Choose the best answer.

1 **a** People should have to get vaccines.
   b People should not have to get vaccines.
2 **a** We should stop all flights from countries that are affected.
   b We should not stop all flights from countries that are affected.
3 **a** It would have a terrible effect on the economy.
   b It would not have a terrible effect on the economy.

PRONUNCIATION FOR LISTENING

Intonation in tag questions

When speakers use tag questions with rising intonation, usually they are uncertain their statement is true. When speakers use tag questions with falling intonation, usually they expect the listener to agree with them. Listening for these differences in intonation can help you understand a speaker's meaning.

Well, people who have the flu should stay home from school or from work, shouldn't they? ↗ (expressing uncertainty)
Well, people who have the flu should stay home from school or from work, shouldn't they? ↘ (expecting agreement)

8 ▶ 3.3 Listen to the sentences. Is the speaker expressing uncertainty or requesting agreement? Write *U* (uncertainty) or *A* (agreement).

1 __U__   4 _____   7 _____
2 __A__   5 _____   8 _____
3 _____   6 _____

PRISM **Digital** Workbook

DISCUSSION

9 Work with a partner. Discuss the questions.

1 Do you think your country is prepared to deal with a pandemic? Why or why not?
2 What would your government do in order to stop a pandemic from occurring?
3 What could you do in a pandemic to protect yourself from contracting a disease?

HEALTH SCIENCE VOCABULARY

1 Read the sentences. Choose the word or phrase that is closest in meaning to the word in bold.

1 Doctors from the organization Doctors Without Borders provide **aid** where it is really needed. For example, many of the doctors work in poor countries.
   a help
   b harm

2 Maha has a bad infection, so her doctor gave her an **antibiotic**.
   a a medication that kills germs
   b a vaccine that prevents disease

3 Most doctors agree that getting a vaccine is the best **prevention**.
   a way to stop a disease from infecting people
   b way to get better if you have a disease

4 This type of flu is very strong; it takes weeks for people to **recover**.
   a get better
   b get worse

5 Some doctors have a personal touch; they prefer to **treat** the person, not just the disease.
   a give food to
   b give medical care to

6 The new drug went through several **trials** before it became available at local drugstores.
   a meetings before a judge
   b tests about effectiveness

7 The pandemic is growing quickly, so the government says the situation is **urgent** because many people could catch the disease.
   a not requiring immediate attention
   b requiring immediate attention

8 The researcher is studying a **virus** that is carried by mosquitoes.
   a organism that causes disease
   b harm or damage to a body part

CONDITIONALS

LANGUAGE

Past unreal conditionals

Past unreal conditionals express situations that were not true in the past. They describe something that was possible but did not happen.

The *if* clause expresses the past unreal condition (the situation that was untrue in the past). The main clause describes an imagined result. Use the past perfect in the *if* clause.

Use *would have* in the main clause to express a predicted result.

if clause	*predicted result*

If she had gone to school that day, she **would have caught** the flu.

Use *could have* or *might have* in the main clause to express something possible or doable.

if clause	*possible result*

If you had gone on your trip, you **might have caught** the virus.

The *if* clause usually comes before the main clause, but it may also follow the main clause.

possible result	*if clause*

The government **could have prevented** a pandemic **if it had acted** in time.

You can use past unreal conditionals to express regrets or sadness.

If I had gotten a vaccine in October, **I wouldn't have caught** the flu this year. (But I didn't, and I regret it.)

2 Complete the interview with a scientist who studies the flu. Use past unreal conditionals with the verbs in parentheses.

PRISM Digital Workbook

Reporter: Today I'm talking to Dr. Julie Niikura, an expert on pandemics. Dr. Niikura, we're all fascinated by the Spanish flu of 1918–1919, I think, because no other pandemic has claimed as many lives — that's at least 40 million people worldwide. What happened?

Dr. Niikura: Well, one problem was that the real cause of the flu was unclear, so there was no flu vaccine at the time. If scientists (1)_____ (develop) a flu vaccine back then, the pandemic (2)_____ (might / not / happen).

Reporter: So, 40 million people (3)_____ (might / survive) if scientists (4)_____ (find) the real cause of the flu?

Dr. Niikura: That's right. In fact, many experts believed that the flu was caused by bacteria, not a virus. So, they focused on developing vaccines for other illnesses caused by bacteria. If they (5)_____ (not / focus) on other illnesses, they (6)_____ (could / discover) more effective ways to prevent the flu. And if more scientists (7)_____ (question) the idea that bacteria was the cause, they (8)_____ (would / realize) the flu was caused by a virus much sooner.

Reporter: Why was it called the Spanish flu?

Dr. Niikura: Well, many countries wouldn't let newspapers report about illnesses and death at the time. But Spain did, so there were a lot more reports there. When King Alfonso XIII got sick, the entire world knew about it. That's why everyone thought the virus was from Spain. If other countries (9)_____ (allow) newspapers to report on it, people (10)_____ (would / not / call) it "Spanish" flu.

Present and future unreal conditionals

Use *present* and *future unreal conditionals* to describe present or future situations that are not true or that are imagined. Use the simple past in the *if* clause. Use the modals *could*, *might*, or *would* in the main clause.

If people **stopped** getting vaccines, there **would be** pandemics.

If people **got** vaccinated, they **could avoid** many illnesses.

Notice that in academic language, speakers use *were* for the verb *be* with all subjects.

If I **were** president, I **would require** everyone to get vaccinated.

If the vaccine **were** available everywhere, fewer outbreaks **would occur**.

PRISM Digital Workbook

3 Complete the sentences about the flu with your own ideas. Use present and future unreal conditionals. If you are writing a main clause, use the modals in parentheses.

1 The flu virus changes every year. If it stayed the same,
  people wouldn't get sick every year . (wouldn't)

2 I didn't get the flu vaccine this year, so I may get sick. _____
  _____ , I wouldn't be worried.

3 There is a warning about a virus outbreak, so people are afraid to travel overseas right now. _____ , they wouldn't be afraid to take their vacations.

4 The virus is not in this country yet, so we don't need a vaccine. If there were an outbreak, _____ . (might)

5 José didn't get the flu vaccine, so he isn't prepared for a flu outbreak. If he had gotten the vaccine, _____ . (would)

LISTENING 2

PREPARING TO LISTEN

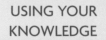

1 Read the definitions. Complete the sentences with the correct form of the words in bold.

> **clinical** (adj) related to medical treatment and tests
> **controlled** (adj) limited
> **data** (n) information or facts about something
> **precaution** (n) an action that is taken to stop something negative from happening
> **prove** (v) to show to be true
> **researcher** (n) a person who studies a subject in detail to discover new information about it
> **scientific** (adj) related to science
> **trial** (n) a test to find out how effective or safe something is

1 Before a new vaccine can be released, experts must _____ that it is safe for public use.
2 First, scientists set up tests in a _____ environment that is appropriate for medical tests. This is often in a lab with advanced medical tools.
3 Then the _____ start to conduct tests on the vaccine.
4 A lot of _____ are taken to make sure the tests are as safe as possible.
5 The tests are performed using _____ methods to ensure accuracy.
6 The tests need to be conducted in _____ conditions so that the results are consistent.
7 The researchers then analyze the _____ collected during the tests.
8 Finally, _____ are conducted with volunteers to test the vaccine before it is released for public use.

2 You are going to listen to a debate about the flu vaccine on a radio program. Before you listen, work with a partner and choose the answers that you think are correct.

1 Experts *agree / don't agree* about whether flu vaccines are necessary.
2 Experts *believe / have proven* that the flu vaccine saves lives.
3 Experts *have / haven't* shown that the flu vaccine is unsafe.
4 *Some / Almost all* of the public choose to get a flu vaccine.

WHILE LISTENING

3 ▶ 3.4 Listen to the introduction and check your answers to Exercise 2.

TAKING NOTES ON MAIN IDEAS

4 ▶ 3.5 Listen to a debate on a radio program. Create a T-chart with one column for Dr. Sandra Smith and one column for Mr. Mark Li. Take notes on each speaker's opinions about the flu vaccine. Use the questions to guide your notes.

- Is the flu vaccine a good idea?
- Do vaccines need to be tested each year?
- Is the flu vaccine helpful or harmful?
- Should people get the flu vaccine? If yes, who?

5 Compare your notes with a partner.

LISTENING FOR DETAILS

6 ▶ 3.5 Write *T* (true) or *F* (false) next to the statements. Then correct the false statements. Listen to the debate again to check your answers.

_____ **1** Millions of people get severely sick from the flu every year.

_____

_____ **2** The majority of the population receives the flu vaccine.

_____

_____ **3** Dr. Smith has gotten the flu vaccine.

_____

_____ **4** Mr. Li is against all forms of vaccination.

_____

_____ **5** There is scientific evidence that the flu vaccine might not work.

_____

_____ **6** There is scientific evidence that the flu vaccine makes people sick.

_____

POST-LISTENING

Strengthening points in an argument

When speakers want to agree or disagree with someone and show that they are right in an argument, they can strengthen or support their point through various techniques, such as:

- offering additional information
- returning to an earlier reference
- repeating the other person's point and saying it is correct
- giving a personal example
- using logic

7 Match each speakers' point to the technique used to strengthen it.

PRISM Digital Workbook

1 All of my colleagues have gotten the vaccine. None of us have caught the flu. _____

2 Dr. Smith is absolutely right that many vaccines work very well and that millions of lives have been saved by vaccination. _____

3 I'd definitely like to challenge the idea that there's no scientific basis for our work. I disagree with Mr. Li on that point. Let me tell you more about my work in that area. _____

4 If people are vaccinated and then they happen to become sick, that doesn't logically mean the vaccine caused the illness. _____

5 Well, I'm sure Dr. Smith is a very good doctor, but I think the flu vaccine package I mentioned earlier is clear. _____

a offering additional information
b returning to an earlier reference
c repeating the other person's point and saying it is correct
d giving a personal example
e using logic

DISCUSSION

8 Work with a partner. Discuss the questions below.

SYNTHESIZING

1 Are vaccines routinely given in your country? Why or why not?

2 When are they given? Who receives them?

3 Based on the debate, has your opinion changed about getting the flu vaccine? Why or why not?

4 Use information from Listening 1 and Listening 2 and your own ideas to answer the following question. Are you for or against vaccines in general? Why or why not?

SPEAKING

CRITICAL THINKING

At the end of this unit, you are going to do the Speaking Task below.

> Role-play a debate between representatives from an international aid organization and representatives from a drug company. Discuss whether or not health care should be free for everyone.

SKILLS

Understanding background and motivation

You can understand more about a speaker's point of view if you know about the person's background, personal and professional motivations, and role in society. This information can also help you prepare your own arguments.

▲ ANALYZE

1 Work with a partner. Read the information about Dr. Sandra Smith and Mr. Mark Li, who debated vaccination in Listening 2, and discuss the questions.

Dr. Sandra Smith is a medical doctor who researches the flu virus at a national university. Some of her research has been paid for by drug companies that manufacture flu vaccines.

Mark Li is an alternative medicine practitioner. He is part of an organization that campaigns against drug companies that make flu vaccines. They believe that the companies create the vaccines to make money and that people don't need them.

1 Why do you think they chose their careers?
2 Who do you think makes more money?
3 What do you think they like best about their work?

2 Compare your answers with another pair. Did you have the same ideas? Why or why not?

3 Read the statements. Who probably said each one? Write *M* (Mark Li) or *S* (Sandra Smith).

1 People who eat the right foods don't need doctors or medicine. _____
2 Modern medicine is one of the greatest achievements of science. _____
3 One day, we'll have a vaccine for the common cold. _____
4 Illness is the body's way of telling you to change your lifestyle. _____
5 Drug companies make too much money from flu vaccines. _____
6 Not giving a patient medication would be against everything I believe. _____

4 Compare your answers with a partner.

5 Work with a partner. Discuss what Mark Li and Sandra Smith might think of the topics. Would they have the same opinions on any of the topics? Support your answer.

APPLY ▲

1 alternative medicine
2 treating diseases with food rather than medicine
3 drug companies advertising their products on television
4 doing exercise to promote health
5 giving a child medicine to reduce a fever or other symptoms of illness
6 free health care for everyone

6 Work in groups:

CREATE ▲

Group A: You work for an international aid organization that sends doctors to help people in developing countries. You believe that health care should be free for everyone.

Group B: You work for a large pharmaceutical company. You believe that health care should not be free for everyone.

In your groups, discuss your background, motivation, and opinions for your side of the issue. Write notes in the table on page 74. Use the following ideas to help you:
• availability of medical care in urban and rural areas
• different types of diseases in certain regions
• the fact that drug companies are businesses and have to make a profit
• issues of fairness for drug companies, individuals, and countries

7 Discuss what you think the other group's background, motivation, and views might be. Write notes in the table below.

	group A	group B
background		
motivation		
opinions		

PREPARATION FOR SPEAKING

USING PERSUASIVE LANGUAGE

When you want to make listeners understand and agree with your point of view, you use *persuasive language*. This calls attention to your main opinions and invites listeners to think about and agree with your point of view. It also makes it more difficult for speakers to disagree with you. Persuasive language can take many forms: giving personal examples, asking challenging questions, presenting support for a position, and addressing the opposing argument. You can also use persuasive words or phrases, such as *How would you feel if*, or strong adverbs or adjectives (*obviously, a lot of*).

Giving personal examples
I've had patients who were healthy, then got the flu vaccine and became sick.

Asking challenging questions
There's plenty of good scientific data that proves that, but let me ask you this: **has the flu vaccine been properly tested?**

Presenting support for a position
The packaging on this flu vaccine clearly states that "**No controlled trials have been performed that demonstrate that this vaccine causes a reduction in influenza.**" It's here in black and white.

Addressing the opposing argument
Let me start by saying that I'm not against all vaccines. **Dr. Smith is absolutely right that many vaccines work very well and that millions of lives have been saved by vaccination.**

1 Match the headings to the examples in the table.

1 give a personal example _____
2 ask challenging questions _____
3 use specific persuasive words and phrases _____
4 give information to support your position _____
5 address the other person's argument _____

a	Have there been proper clinical trials to prove that it works, that it stops infection?
b	However, the flu can cause severe illness or worse for a small percentage of the people who get it. It may not sound like a lot, but actually this is hundreds of thousands of people around the world each year.
	There isn't one single scientific study that proves that this year's flu vaccine works.
c	So while Mr. Li is right – we don't do clinical trials of the flu vaccine in the way that we do trials for other medicines – that doesn't mean we aren't scientific in our methods.
d	All my colleagues have gotten the vaccine. None of us have caught the flu.
	Let me tell you more about my work in that area.
e	*Obviously*, we want to do everything in our power to stop the infection from spreading.
	Supposing you gave your kids the vaccine and it made them worse rather than better?
	How would you feel if someone in your family did not get the vaccine and then became really sick?
	It's obvious that the vaccine hasn't been properly tested.

2 Work with a partner. Rewrite the facts as persuasive statements. Use the strategy in parentheses to help you.

1 Some big pharmaceutical companies spend more money on advertising than on research and development. (support for a position)

_____

_____

2 The cost of developing a new vaccine is $1.5 billion. (use persuasive words and phrases)

_____

_____

3 It takes years of study to become a doctor, which is why they are among the highest-paid professional workers. (give a personal example)

_____

_____

4 The top five global drug companies are wealthier than many of the world's nations. (ask challenging questions)

_____

_____

5 Malaria is an easily preventable disease, but people still contract it because they can't pay for a vaccine. (address the opposing argument)

_____

_____

3 Read your statements to another pair. Are their statements persuasive? Why or why not?

SPEAKING TASK

Role-play a debate between representatives from an international aid organization and representatives from a drug company. Discuss whether or not health care should be free for everyone.

PREPARE

1 Separate into your two groups. Look back at your notes on each group's background, motivation, and opinions in Critical Thinking. Add any new information.

2 Prepare an opening statement for the debate to introduce your viewpoint. Review the language in Preparation for Speaking to express your opinions. Practice your opening statement in your group. Make sure each person makes at least one comment.

3 Think about the other group's views and make notes about how they respond to your opening statement. Make notes of persuasive language that you might use to counter their arguments. Remember to:

- give personal examples and opinions (if possible)
- ask challenging questions
- give information to support your viewpoint

4 Prepare for the debate.

- Be ready to make notes on what the other group says, as you will need to respond to their views in your counterargument.
- Use your ideas from Exercise 3 to help you.
- Use the following format for the debate:

Group A: Announce the topic: *Health care should be free for everyone.*
Group A: Opening statement in favor
Group B: Opening statement against
Group A: Counterargument in favor
Group B: Counterargument against

5 Refer to the Task Checklist below as you prepare for your debate.

TASK CHECKLIST	✔
State and support your position in the debate clearly.	
Ask challenging questions.	
Give personal examples.	
Address the other group's argument.	
Use persuasive language.	

DISCUSS

6 Have the debate with another group.

7 Answer these questions.

1 What did you like about the way arguments were presented?
2 What could be improved?
3 Which argument do you think was the most persuasive? Why?

CITING SOURCES IN A PRESENTATION

PREPARING TO LISTEN

SKILLS

Citing sources

When you are giving a presentation or participating in a debate, your arguments will sound stronger if you use facts, statistics, and quotes from outside sources, such as reputable experts or organizations.

When you use sources in an academic presentation, you should:

- cite (say clearly) where the information came from: an article, a video, a book, etc.
- put the quotation in your own words
- name the author or organization that published the information
- give enough information so that the audience can find the exact source

1 Work with a partner and answer the questions.

1 What kinds of sources could you use in a debate about health-care costs?
2 Have you used sources in an academic paper or a presentation?
3 What should you always do when you use someone else's ideas in an academic assignment? Why?

WHILE LISTENING

2 ▶ 3.6 You are going to hear excerpts from three presentations. Listen and note the cited information that comes from another source.

	cited information (quote, statistic, etc.)	person or organization	title of book or report	date of book or report
1				
2				
3				

3 ▶ 3.6 Listen again and check (✔) which details are given for each source.

PRACTICE

> **Ways to introduce source information**
>
> **In a book published by** Meridian House Press in 2012, Dr. Manuel
> Fernandes **argues that** ...
> **According to** Doctors Without Borders ...
> **A recent report by** the World Health Organization **found that** ...

4 Complete the citations with the words in the box.

A recent report	According to	found	In his book	points out

1 _____ *Pathologies of Power*, published by University of California
Press in 2003, Dr. Paul Farmer _____ that ...
2 _____ statistics from the Centers for Disease Control, ...
3 _____ by Rebecca Siegel and her colleagues at the American
Cancer Society _____ that ...

5 Paraphrase each of the sources below. Then introduce them as you would
in a presentation.

1 "Observers have noted that, on average, physicians interrupt patients
within 18 seconds of when they begin telling their story."
Groopman, Jerome. *How Doctors Think*. New York: Houghton
Mifflin, 2007.
2 "During recent flu seasons, between 80% and 90% of flu-related deaths
have occurred in people 65 years and older."
"Key Facts about Seasonal Flu Vaccine." United States Centers for
Disease Control and Prevention (CDC), May 2016, www.cdc.gov.
3 "Modern medicine is a negation of health. It isn't organized to serve
human health, but only itself, as an institution. It makes more people
sick than it heals."
– Ivan Illich (Austrian philosopher, 1926–2002)

REAL-WORLD APPLICATION

6 Choose one or more of the statements below. Go online to find a source
that supports the statement. Paraphrase the source. Then present the
information as you would in a class presentation.

1 Pharmaceutical companies spend a lot of money on advertising.
2 Many lives have been saved by the flu vaccine.
3 Many people are using alternative medicine such as homeopathy.
4 Exercise promotes health.

Listening skills	Distinguish main ideas from details; take notes on main ideas and details
Pronunciation	Sentence stress
Speaking skills	Give background information; signposting
Speaking Task	Give a presentation about a change in the environment
On Campus	Time management

ACTIVATE YOUR KNOWLEDGE

Work with a partner. Discuss the questions.

1 What is deforestation?

2 What are its causes and effects?

3 Other than deforestation, what things do people do that affect the environment?

4 How can people use natural resources without harming the environment?

PREPARING TO WATCH

ACTIVATING YOUR KNOWLEDGE

1 Work with a partner. Discuss the questions.

1 Can you think of any animals that have disappeared or are endangered?
2 What role do humans play in making an animal extinct or endangered?
3 What can people do to prevent more animals from becoming extinct?

PREDICTING CONTENT USING VISUALS

2 Look at the pictures from the video. Discuss the questions with your partner.

1 What type of animal do you see in the first picture?
2 What do you think the doctors and scientists are doing?
3 What kind of animal is behind the female reporter? What do you know about it?

GLOSSARY

clone (v) to produce a cell or organism that has the same chemical patterns in its cells as the original from which it was artificially produced

skin cell (n) the smallest unit of an animal that makes up skin

genetic (adj) relating to the biological process by which the characteristics of living things are passed from generation to generation

euthanize (v) to kill an animal because it is very old or sick

astonishing (adj) very surprising

counterpart (n) a person or thing that has the same position or purpose as another person or thing

---

WHILE WATCHING

3 ▶ Watch the video. Which sentence best summarizes the main idea?

a Bantengs, which are endangered, have been cloned by using the cells of an animal that died 23 years earlier.

b We now have the technology to clone endangered species, but this has many people concerned that we aren't dealing with the real problem.

c While certain animals cannot be cloned at this time, it is possible that we may be able to clone them in the future.

4 ▶ Watch again. Answer the questions.

1 Why do scientists believe that they are closer to protecting endangered species?

_____

2 How were scientists able to clone the banteng?

_____

3 What worries some conservationists about cloning?

_____

5 Work with a partner. Discuss the questions.

1 Based on the information in the video, how successful is cloning? Explain your answer.

2 Do you think cloned animals are able to thrive in the wild? Why or why not?

3 What are the dangers of cloning?

4 How might cloning affect the environment?

DISCUSSION

6 Work in a small group. Discuss the questions.

1 Are there any endangered species in your country or region? Which ones?

2 What are people currently doing to help save these animals?

3 In your opinion, is cloning a good method to save endangered species? Why or why not?

4 In addition to trying to protect endangered species, what other ways are people in your community helping the environment?

UNDERSTANDING MAIN IDEAS

UNDERSTANDING DETAILS

MAKING INFERENCES

LISTENING

LISTENING 1

PREPARING TO LISTEN

UNDERSTANDING
KEY VOCABULARY

1 You are going to listen to a lecture about habitat destruction. Before you listen, read the text and write the words in bold next to the definitions.

> **Conservation** of our **coastal** regions is now vital as the destruction of this **habitat** is causing the extinction of many plant and animal species. This is the result of **waste** and pollution from the way we constantly **exploit** the habitat for its resources. The plants and animals cannot **adapt** to the changes humans make to their habitat. If humans continue to **modify** the environment, the **impact** on plants and animals will worsen.

1 _____ (n) the protection of plants, animals, and natural areas
2 _____ (n) the natural surroundings where a plant or animal lives
3 _____ (n) unwanted matter or material
4 _____ (adj) on or related to land by the sea or ocean
5 _____ (v) to adjust to different conditions
6 _____ (v) to use something unfairly for your own advantage
7 _____ (n) the strong effect that something has on something else
8 _____ (v) to change something to make it more acceptable or less extreme

Distinguishing main ideas from details

Speakers often support their main ideas with details. Listening for main ideas and details can help you understand a speaker's meaning. To determine if a speaker's words are main ideas or details, ask yourself: Is this an important point, or does it support an important point?

PRISM **Digital** Workbook

2 Label each group of sentences (group A and group B) *main ideas* or *details*.

group A _____
1 Planet Earth is dynamic and always changing. _____
2 Sometimes, natural forces can destroy the environment. _____
3 However, humans are also responsible for a lot of habitat destruction. _____
4 Humans haven't only affected the land and its animals, they have also affected the sea. _____
5 One other animal that is as at home in the city and in the countryside is the raccoon. _____
6 Not everyone feels that ecotourism is actually helping the environment. _____

group B _____
a Pollution from coastal cities has damaged the ocean.
b In Europe, only about 15% of land hasn't been modified by humans.
c Just 10,000 years ago, about half of the planet was covered in ice.
d In 1991, a volcano in the Philippines erupted and killed many people and animals.
e Tourists who travel long distances by airplane create pollution.
f The number of city raccoons has increased.

3 Match the main ideas in Exercise 2 to the details that support them.

WHILE LISTENING

4 ▶ 4.1 Listen to the lecture and check your answers.

LISTENING FOR
MAIN IDEAS

Taking notes on main ideas and details

One way to take notes is to list main ideas on one half of the paper and details that support them on the other side of the paper. You do not need to write complete sentences. You should listen for key words and important information.

5 ▶ **4.1** Listen to the lecture again and complete the notes with details you hear.

Earth is always changing	10,000 years ago, about half of Earth covered in ice; now only (1)_____ is covered in ice.
	Changes are in part due to (2)_____ rather than human causes.
Natural forces can destroy the environment	1991 – volcano in the Philippines erupted and killed many people and animals; destroyed (3)_____ of farmland and a huge area of forest
	Caused severe floods when (4)_____ by volcanic ash
Humans are also responsible for habitat destruction	Originally more than (5)_____ square miles of rainforest worldwide; less than (6)_____ today
	Deforestation: approximately 1,722,225 square feet per year
	In Europe, only about 15% of land not modified by humans
	Some places have habitat broken into parts, e.g., separated by roads – called (7)_____
	can cause serious problems
Humans have affected the land, animals, and sea	Pollution from coastal cities has damaged the ocean; destroyed habitat of (8)_____
Animals are feeling at home in the city and in the countryside	Monkeys live alongside humans in (9)_____
	In (10)_____, coyotes in urban areas
	Leopards in (11)_____
	Number of city raccoons increased
	Have different (12)_____ depending on their environment; common foods include (13)_____; raccoons in cities eat (14)_____
Not everyone feels that ecotourism is helping the environment	Tourists travel long distances by airplane, create (15)_____
	Resorts use local (16)_____ such as water and produce
	(17)_____ that creates pollution in the local environment

a leopard in the streets of Mumbai

6 Use your notes from Exercise 5 to complete the text.

SUMMARIZING

> The Earth always changes. ⁽¹⁾_____ years ago, half of it was covered in ice. Humans have changed the Earth; originally there were more than six million square miles of ⁽²⁾_____ , today there are less than ⁽³⁾_____ million. Each year, about ⁽⁴⁾_____ square feet are destroyed. Raccoons exploit the city environment by eating ⁽⁵⁾_____ . Critics of ecotourism say air travel and waste from hotels cause ⁽⁶⁾_____ .

POST-LISTENING

7 Read each excerpt from the lecture. Circle the statement that best matches the lecturer's opinion.

LISTENING FOR OPINION

  1 "Part of this environmental change is due to natural, rather than human, causes."
    a Natural causes result in some environmental change.
    b Natural causes result in most environmental change.
    c Human causes result in most environmental change.
  2 "Habitat destruction hasn't been bad news for all animals."
    a The destruction of animal habitats is always a bad thing.
    b The destruction of animal habitats is not necessarily negative.
    c The destruction of animal habitats is inevitable.
  3 "We tend to think of human activity as always having a negative impact on the environment."
    a It's common to think that humans only negatively affect the environment.
    b It's wrong to think that humans only negatively affect the environment.
    c It's correct to think that humans only negatively affect the environment.

PRONUNCIATION FOR LISTENING

Sentence stress

In English, stressing different words can change the meaning or the focus of a sentence. Speakers often place more stress on key words, such as nouns, verbs, adjectives, and adverbs. Other times, they place more stress on words they want you to notice.

<u>Conservationists</u> want to protect the environment. (The speaker stresses *who* wants to protect the environment.)

Conservationists want to <u>protect</u> the environment. (The speaker stresses *what* conservationists want to do.)

PRISM Digital Workbook

8 ▶ 4.2 Listen to the sentence starters and underline the words the speaker stresses. The first two are done for you.

1 Sometimes, <u>natural forces</u> destroy animal habitats …
2 <u>Sometimes</u>, natural forces destroy animal habitats …
3 Humans have changed the Earth …
4 Humans have changed the Earth …
5 Humans have changed the Earth …
6 Humans have changed the Earth …

9 Match the sentence endings with the sentence starters in Exercise 8. Pay attention to word stress.

a … but animals haven't changed it too much. __4__
b … but most of the time they don't. _____
c … but they haven't changed the sun. _____
d … and you can't say that they haven't. _____
e … rather than humans. _____
f … and in some cases they've improved it. _____

10 Work with a partner. Practice saying the complete sentences.

DISCUSSION

11 Work with a partner. Discuss the questions.

1 How have people changed habitats in the country you live in?
2 Think of an environment you know. Which animals live there naturally? Do any animals live there that are originally from somewhere else?

⊙ LANGUAGE DEVELOPMENT

MULTI-WORD PREPOSITIONS

Multi-word prepositions are two- or three-word phrases that function like one-word prepositions, such as *of*, *on*, or *by*. Multi-word prepositions include:

- two-word phrases (*apart from*, *according to*)
- three-word phrases (*by means of*, *as well as*)

Like one-word prepositions, multi-word prepositions are followed by nouns, noun phrases, and gerunds. They show the relationship between two things. For example, *in front of* shows location.

1 Match the multi-word prepositions to the functions.

1 according to, based on	**a** making an exception
2 owing to, due to	**b** giving a source
3 apart from, except for	**c** giving another choice
4 together with, as well as	**d** including
5 rather than, instead of	**e** giving a reason

2 Circle the correct multi-word preposition to complete each sentence.

1 *Based on / Apart from* research that I carried out in Ethiopia, I can conclude that the destruction of deserts can be reversed.

2 Visitors rarely go to the research station *according to / due to* its extremely remote location.

3 *According to / Rather than* the latest *Economist Magazine*, share prices fell sharply last month.

4 The engineers decided to use solar power *owing to / instead of* conventional batteries.

5 The doctors used strong medication *as well as / except for* lots of liquid to help cure the patients.

6 The phone is assembled almost entirely by machines, *instead of / except for* the outer case.

3 Write your own sentences. Use a multi-word preposition with the function in parentheses.

1 (giving a source) _____

2 (giving a reason) _____

3 (giving another choice) _____

4 (including) _____

5 (making an exception) _____

THE PAST PERFECT

The *past perfect* is used to describe a completed event or time period that happened before another event in the past. Use the simple past to describe the later event or time period.

Police officers spotted a young leopard in the streets of Mumbai. The leopard **had moved** into the city from the nearby forest.
(First, the leopard moved into the city from the forest; then the police spotted it.)

Form the past perfect with *had* + the past participle of the main verb. Form the negative by adding *not* after *had*. The form is the same for all subjects.
cover → had covered / had not covered (hadn't covered)

You can use the prepositions *before, by,* and *until* to introduce the later time period.
Until these natural resources were discovered, of course, changes to desert habitats **had not** really **affected** people very much.

People often use the past perfect to give reasons or background information for later events.
Before people started settling in the Arctic, much of the land **had been** untouched.

PRISM Digital Workbook

4 ▶ 4.3 Listen to an excerpt from a student's report on Rachel Carson. Complete the text with the simple past or past perfect verbs you hear.

Before she (1)_____ her influential book *Silent Spring* in 1962, Rachel Carson (2)_____ years working for the U.S. government at environmental agencies like the U.S. Bureau of Fisheries and the U.S. Fish and Wildlife Service. During her time there, she (3)_____ her own personal research and writing. By 1955, Carson (4)_____ already _____ several books on environmental research when she (5)_____ to do research full-time. One subject that she was particularly interested in was the effects of pesticides[1] on the environment and on human health. During World War II, the government (6)_____ the pesticide DDT to protect people against diseases caused by pests. After the war, farmers (7)_____ large amounts of DDT into the air to protect their crops. Carson (8)_____ that the chemical was making people sick with cancer and was causing other animals to die, so she (9)_____ to do scientific research on the subject and publish it as a book to warn people about the risks. After Carson (10)_____ *Silent Spring*, the pesticide industry (11)_____ her for her research. However, the U.S. government (12)_____ by banning the use of DDT in the United States. Soon her book was translated into several languages and was published around the world.

[1]**pesticides** (n) chemicals used to kill pests like insects and small animals

Rachel Carson

5 Complete the sentences with the past perfect or the simple past form of the verbs in parentheses.

1 Before people _____ (settle) in the northernmost parts of the Arctic, the area _____ (be) mostly empty.

2 Before the city _____ (begin) developing the area for new residential buildings, people _____ (used) it as a park.

3 We _____ (not/notice) coyotes coming into in this neighborhood until we _____ (see) news reports about them on TV.

4 By the time the volcano _____ (erupt), the government _____ (evacuate) everyone from the area.

5 Until the city _____ (create) a committee to clean up the local environment, the parks and streets _____ (be) completely covered in trash.

VERBS TO DESCRIBE ENVIRONMENTAL CHANGE

6 Read the definitions. Complete the sentences with the correct form of the words in bold.

> **adapt** (v) to adjust to different conditions
> **affect** (v) to have an influence on something
> **decline** (v) to gradually become less, worse, or lower
> **exploit** (v) to use something for an advantage
> **extract** (v) to remove or take out something
> **impact** (n) the strong effect or influence something has on a situation or person
> **occur** (v) to happen
> **survive** (v) to continue to live or exist

1 Coyotes have _____ to living in cities, and now they are doing well there.

2 Extinct species could have _____ if people had taken more care to protect them.

3 The number of wild raccoons in New York has _____ over many years.

4 Resources have been _____ from endangered habitats without destroying them.

5 Humans have had a negative _____ on the environment by destroying forests and using dangerous chemicals.

6 Changes to the environment can negatively _____ animals.

7 Many environmental changes have _____ because of people's actions.

8 Urban raccoons have _____ their new habitat by finding food in people's garbage.

USING YOUR
KNOWLEDGE

UNDERSTANDING
KEY VOCABULARY

PRISM Digital
Workbook

PREPARING TO LISTEN

1 Work with a partner. Discuss the questions.

1 What is a desert?
2 Are there any desert areas in your country? If so, where are they?
3 What kinds of plants, animals, or products come from the desert?

2 You are going to listen to a talk about desert habitats. Before you listen, read the sentences and write the words in bold next to the definitions.

1 Alaska usually has a **harsh** winter with extremely cold temperatures.
2 Yosemite National Park is a **wilderness** area, protected by the Parks Department. Visitors are not allowed to interact with the wildlife there.
3 Researchers collected **minerals** to find out more about what is in the soil.
4 **Diamond** is the hardest naturally occurring substance on Earth.
5 The electric company installed **copper** wires in the new building.
6 Many countries use **natural gas** found below the Earth's surface to heat their homes.
7 The government has banned coal **mining** in certain areas where it could be extremely dangerous to the environment.

a _____ (n) the industry or activity of removing valuable substances from the earth
b _____ (n) fuel for heating or cooking that is found underground
c _____ (n) natural substances found in the earth such as coal or gold
d _____ (n) a very hard, valuable stone, often used in jewelry
e _____ (adj) severe and unpleasant
f _____ (n) a place that is in a completely natural state without houses, industry, roads, etc.
g _____ (n) a reddish-brown metal, used in electrical equipment and for making wires and coins

WHILE LISTENING

3 ▶ **4.4** Listen to the talk. Complete the notes on the main ideas.

Topic: (1)_____

Humans have learned to (2)_____ the resources of
the desert

The desert is an (3)_____ that supports a variety of plant
and animal life

If desert is destroyed:

    (4)_____ will be saltier.

    Plants will (5)_____ ; we'll lose a valuable food source

    More (6)_____ will be in the air.

Solutions: (7)_____ desert resources carefully instead of
abusing them; apply (8)_____ solutions

4 ▶ **4.4** Listen again. Number the details in the order you hear them.

  a Bringing water into the desert to grow plants can make desert soil too salty. _____

  b Computer technology can forecast how climate change will affect deserts. _____

  c The Earth's deserts cover 13 million square miles. _____

  d Scientists are using solar energy to produce water in deserts. _____

  e The Topnaar people have an understanding of the natural world. _____

  f Deserts provide many of the world's minerals and metals. _____

  g There are over 2,200 desert plant species in Saudi Arabia. _____

  h Desert surface temperatures in summer can reach 175°F (80°C). _____

5 ▶ **4.4** Answer the questions with a partner. Then listen again to check your answers.

  1 What percent of the Earth's surface is desert? _____

  2 In which part of Africa do the Bedouins live? _____

  3 What minerals are found in the desert? _____

  4 What conditions are needed for acacia trees to grow?

    _____

  5 What is one of the best-known desert animals in the Arabian Peninsula?

    _____

  6 What kind of energy are scientists in Saudi Arabia using to produce fresh water? _____

POST-LISTENING

6 Match the parts of a talk to the sentences from the talk.

1 giving background information _____
2 explaining a problem _____
3 offering a solution _____

a The problem is that human activity is affecting modern deserts. According to the United Nations, traditional ways of life are changing as human activities such as cattle ranching, farming, and large-scale tourism grow.

b The United Nations reports in *Global Deserts Outlook* that the Earth's deserts cover about 13 million square miles, or 25% of the Earth's surface.

c The UN gives the example of using the latest computer technology to help forecast how climate change will affect deserts and using that information to prepare for these changes.

7 Read the three details. Which part of the talk do they come from? Write *background information, explain a problem,* or *offer a solution.*

a Tribes such as the Topnaar, in southwestern Africa, are known for their ability to survive in the desert due to their use of local plants and animals for food, medicine, and clothing. _____

b According to the blog *A Smarter Planet*, scientists in Saudi Arabia are already using solar energy to produce fresh water in the desert.

_____

c Data from the United Nations shows that every year, nearly 2% of healthy desert disappears. _____

DISCUSSION

8 Work with a partner. Discuss the questions.

1 What natural habitats exist in your country?
2 What human activities take place in those habitats?
3 Do you use any products or foods that come from those habitats?
4 Use your notes from Listening 1 and Listening 2 to answer the following questions. Do you live in an urban, suburban, or rural area? What is the environment like? What animals live there? How has it changed over time?

SPEAKING

CRITICAL THINKING

At the end of this unit, you are going to do the Speaking Task below.

> Give a presentation about a change in the environment and discuss possible solutions.

SKILLS

Organizing information in a presentation

Understanding the organization of information in a presentation can help you understand the development of the speaker's ideas. An outline is a general plan of the features you will include in a presentation. Outlines are useful ways to show the connection between main points, specific examples, and details.

1 Look back at your notes from Listening 2. Complete the outline for Listening 2 with the phrases from the box. Then compare with a partner.

ANALYZE

PRISM Digital Workbook

> Human survival   Desert environment and wildlife   People in cities
> Desert plants   People in deserts   Desert animals
> Use wind and solar energy   Plant and animal survival

Topic: Decline and destruction of deserts
Introduction (background information): _____
I. Main idea: _____
   A. Detail: _____
      a. Example: Topnaar
      b. Example: Bedouins
   B. Detail: _____
II. Main idea: _____
   A. Detail: _____
      a. Example: Acacia tree
   B. Detail: _____
      a. Example: Arabian oryx
Solutions: Manage desert resources carefully instead of abusing them; apply technological solutions; _____ to provide clean energy in existing desert cities

2 Look at the outline again and write *T* (true) or *F* (false) next to the statements.

The outline ...

_____ 1 shows clear connections between the presentation topic, main ideas, examples, and supporting details.

_____ 2 shows the order of the parts in the presentation.

_____ 3 tells the speaker exactly what to say in the presentation.

_____ 4 includes irrelevant details that do not belong in the talk.

3 Create an outline for a talk on one of the topics below. Choose a topic, do some research online, and prepare an outline. Use the outline from Exercise 1 as a model. Be sure to include two or three main ideas with details and examples in your outline. You will use this outline for the Speaking Task at the end of this unit.

increase in "super storms" (extreme hurricanes) around the world

ice melting in the Arctic

destruction of the Amazon rainforest

4 Think of some possible solutions to the problem you chose in Exercise 3. Write notes about them in your outline.

PREPARATION FOR SPEAKING

GIVING BACKGROUND INFORMATION

> *Background information* is often necessary to put a problem in context. In other words, you need to say *why* it is a problem. One way of structuring this background information is to give main ideas, examples of those ideas, and details to clarify the examples:
>
> Let's begin by looking at some background information from the United Nations Environment Programme. The United Nations reports in *Global Deserts Outlook* that ...
>
> Humans have learned to exploit the resources of the desert for survival and profit by adapting their behavior, culture, and technology to this harsh environment. To give you an example, tribes such as the Topnaar ...

1 Match the sentences with their functions.

1 According to the Food and Agriculture Organization of the United Nations, millions of people around the world survive by eating fish. _____
2 Data show that the amount of manmade chemicals in the oceans is increasing. Eighty percent of ocean pollution comes from human activity on land. _____
3 If we continue to pollute the world's oceans, marine plants and animals will not survive. _____
4 Oceans are essential for life on Earth. People rely on them for survival. _____
5 All of us who rely on the oceans for food will then have to find different food sources. _____
6 Human activity is destroying oceans all over the world. The two main problems are pollution and overfishing. _____

a introduces the background information
b gives a specific detail that illustrates the background information
c says what the main problem is
d gives details that explain the problem
e explains the consequences of the problem
f says how the problem might affect the audience personally

SIGNPOSTING

Speakers *signpost* by using transitional words and phrases in lectures and presentations. This helps them guide the listener through what they are saying now, and what they will say next. You can use signposting throughout your talk to help the audience understand the talk's structure, such as when you are giving an example, starting a new topic, or giving a conclusion. Here are examples of signposting language:

- to give an example: *For example, To illustrate*
- to start a new topic: *Next, Now I'm going to talk about*
- to give a conclusion: *In conclusion, To sum up*

PRISM **Digital** Workbook

2 Read these sentences. Match the signposting phrases in bold to their functions.

1 But **what does this mean** for the rest of the world? _____
2 **To put it another way**, we will all be affected. _____
3 **Moving on to** the typical desert environment, ... _____
4 **A good example of this** is Egyptian cotton. _____
5 **That's all I have to say** on that point. _____
6 **Let's begin by** looking at background information from the United Nations Environment Programme. _____
7 **To summarize**, deserts are not only important to the people who live in them ... _____
8 **The topic of my talk** is the decline and destruction of the world's deserts. _____

a introducing the topic
b giving an overview
c finishing a section
d starting a new section

e querying and analyzing
f giving examples
g paraphrasing and clarifying
h summarizing and concluding

3 Match the signposting language to the functions from Exercise 2.

1 That concludes this part of the talk ... _____
2 To give you an example ... _____
3 Let's turn now to ... _____
4 I'd like to recap ... _____
5 Today I'm going to talk about ... _____
6 Let's consider this in more detail ... _____
7 So what I'm saying is ... _____
8 I have three main points to make ... _____

SPEAKING TASK

▶ Give a presentation about a change in the environment and discuss possible solutions.

PREPARE

1 Look back at the outline for the research you did in Critical Thinking. Add any new information you would like to include.

2 Prepare a short introduction. Make notes based on your research from Critical Thinking. Think about what kind of background information to include in your introduction so that the audience understands the problems in your presentation. Use language from Preparation for Speaking to help you.

3 Look back at your proposed solutions in your outline. What kind of information could you include in your conclusion? Use signposting language from Preparation for Speaking to help you.

4 Refer to the Task Checklist below as you prepare your presentation.

TASK CHECKLIST	✔
Use signposting language to help guide the audience.	
Give background information.	
Explain the problem and possible solutions.	
Stress words for emphasis.	

PRESENT

5 Form a group and take turns giving your presentations. Take notes as you listen to your classmates' presentations. Ask questions at the end of each presentation.

6 Were the other students' presentations similar to your own? Why or why not?

ON CAMPUS

TIME MANAGEMENT

PREPARING TO LISTEN

SKILLS

When people *procrastinate*, they keep delaying something that must be done, often because it is unpleasant or boring. It's easy for college students to procrastinate. Learn strategies to avoid procrastination.

1 Work with a partner. Discuss the questions.

1 Do you procrastinate, or do you usually plan enough time to get things done?
2 What are some reasons that college students procrastinate?

WHILE LISTENING

2 ▶ 4.5 Listen to the news report. Answer the questions.

1 What percentage of students procrastinate?
2 What reasons do they give?
3 What do they do instead of doing schoolwork?
4 What are some strategies that students can use to avoid procrastinating?

3 ▶ 4.5 Match the sentence halves. Then listen again and check your answers.

1 1,300 students
2 87% of the students
3 45% of the procrastinators
4 Male students tend to
5 Female students tend to
6 Both male and female students
7 Both male and female students

a feel overwhelmed.
b watch videos or use social media instead of studying.
c should learn strategies to help them manage their time.
d procrastinate because they don't like schoolwork.
e procrastinate on their schoolwork.
f say that procrastination has a negative effect.
g took the survey.

PRACTICE

4 Here are some ways for students to stop procrastinating. Read the suggestions carefully. Choose the three pieces of advice that you feel are most useful.

1 Know when you procrastinate the most, what kind of work you avoid, and why.
2 Divide a project up into smaller parts, and do one small part at a time.
3 Start with a job that is fun, easy, or interesting.
4 If you feel overwhelmed, finish what you are doing and stop.
5 Pay attention to what you have done, not what you still have to do.
6 Be realistic about how much time a project will take.
7 Know when you feel most energetic and use that time for the work you enjoy least.
8 Choose a comfortable place to study where there are no distractions.
9 Use apps that block social media and turn off your phone.
10 Find resources at your college to help with time management.

5 Work with a partner and compare your answers. Say why you think the advice is useful. Use examples from your own experience.

REAL-WORLD APPLICATION

6 You are going to conduct a survey to find out how much your classmates procrastinate and what strategies they use to get work done. Work in groups of four or five students. Choose one question each.

1 How do you approach a major project or school assignment?
2 How often do you put off doing homework or assignments?
3 What kinds of work do you often avoid doing? Why?
4 What strategies do you use to get work done?
5 What time of day are you most productive? Why?

7 Ask your question to as many people as possible. Make a note of the responses.

8 Report your findings to your group. Then answer the questions below.

1 What generalizations can you make about your classmates' time management strategies?
2 What strategies might help the most people?

LEARNING OBJECTIVES

Listening skills	Understand figurative language; understand strong and tentative suggestions
Pronunciation	Emphasis in contrasting opinions; emphasize a word or idea to signal a problem
Speaking skill	Identify problems and suggest solutions
Speaking Task	Discuss a housing problem and possible solutions
On Campus	Understand college expectations

ARCHITECTURE

ACTIVATE YOUR KNOWLEDGE

Work with a partner. Discuss the questions.

1 Where do you think this building is?
2 Who do you think might use the building? What is it used for?
3 What do you think the advantages of the building are?
The disadvantages?

WATCH AND LISTEN

PREPARING TO WATCH

ACTIVATING YOUR
KNOWLEDGE

1 Look at the example in the table. Think of three more famous buildings or structures and use them to complete the table. Then compare your answers with a partner.

building / structure	location	features
The Eiffel Tower	Paris, France	tall, beautiful, romantic

PREDICTING CONTENT
USING VISUALS

2 Look at the pictures from the video. Discuss the questions with your partner.

1 Compare and contrast the buildings in the first photo and in the second photo.
2 How have buildings changed since the first skyscrapers were built?
3 Which view do you prefer, the view in the third photo or the view in the fourth photo? Why?

> **GLOSSARY**
>
> **stately** (adj) formal in style and appearance
>
> **consumer** (n) a person who buys goods or services for their own use
>
> **market** (n) the business of buying or selling a particular product or service
>
> **skyline** (n) the shape of objects against the sky, especially buildings in a city
>
> **bar chart** (n) a graph in which different amounts are represented by vertical or horizontal rectangles that have the same width but different heights or lengths

WHILE WATCHING

3 ▶ Watch the video. Write *T* (true) or *F* (false) next to the statements below. Correct the false statements.

_____ 1 Skyscrapers originated in New York City.

_____ 2 Louis Sullivan is credited with creating the skyscraper.

_____ 3 The first skyscraper was completed in 1898.

_____ 4 The skyscraper is considered a symbol of American consumerism in the world economy.

_____ 5 Skyscrapers have changed the appearance of cities around the world.

UNDERSTANDING MAIN IDEAS

4 ▶ Watch again. Complete the notes.

Architects began to experiment with new buildings after:
(1)_____

Where Louis Sullivan lived and worked: (2)_____

Where Auditorium Building is located: (3)_____

In 1920, 100 million consumers were served by: (4)_____

Tall buildings represent: (5)_____

UNDERSTANDING DETAILS

5 Work with a partner and discuss the questions.

1 How have other disasters influenced building and building styles?

2 What other factors affect a building's design?

3 What do you think inspires great architects like Louis Sullivan?

MAKING INFERENCES

DISCUSSION

6 Discuss the questions with your partner.

1 Are there skyscrapers in your city? How are they similar to or different from the skyscrapers in the video?

2 What materials are often used in skyscrapers?

3 Is there a famous building that represents the culture of your country? What does it symbolize to you?

LISTENING

LISTENING 1

PREPARING TO LISTEN

1 You are going to listen to a conversation between two property developers. Before you listen, read the sentences and write the correct form of the words in bold next to the definitions.

1 Many people believe real estate is a good **investment** because you make money when you sell it.

2 Selina prefers houses from the eighteenth century, but I prefer **contemporary** houses that have a lot of windows and glass.

3 The house we want to buy is old, but it has a lot of **potential** to look like new again.

4 José said he could **transform** the old house into something that looked like new with just a few small construction projects.

5 Sandra **obtained** ownership of the building after paying the previous owner $1.5 million.

6 The building has some beautiful architectural **features**, such as a green space and very old sculptures on the roof.

7 The construction did not start well. A piece of the wall **collapsed** and had to be rebuilt.

8 I **anticipate** that the houses will rise in value in the next ten years.

a _____ (v) to change the appearance of something

b _____ (v) to fall down suddenly

c _____ (adj) happening now; modern

d _____ (n) a noticeable or important characteristic or part

e _____ (v) to expect that something will happen

f _____ (n) someone's or something's ability to develop, achieve, or succeed

g _____ (v) to get something, especially by a planned effort

h _____ (n) money that is put into something in order to make a profit

2 Work with a partner. Discuss the questions.

1 Do you prefer older or more contemporary buildings? Explain your reasons.

2 Describe a building that you like. Why do you like it?

WHILE LISTENING

3 ▶ 5.1 Listen to the conversation. What two problems are discussed?

LISTENING FOR
MAIN IDEAS

1 _____

2 _____

4 ▶ 5.1 Listen again. Complete the notes on the proposed solutions to
the problems. Then compare answers with a partner.

TAKING NOTES
ON DETAILS

Solutions

1 Nearby _____ and restoration will _____ the area

2 Tear down the original building

3 _____ the building; it has lots of _____

4 Transform _____ with a _____ building

5 Design new building with _____ features

6 Add _____ landmark made of _____ and _____

7 Include pieces of _____ and red _____ from old _____
as part of new _____

8 Put _____ on the ground floor and _____ or _____ above

5 Use your notes from Exercise 4 to correct the statements.

1 At the beginning of the conversation, both developers
think a building development in Westside is a good idea.

2 There isn't any development going on in Westside.

3 There has been a lot of investment in the area in the
past 20 years.

4 The developers think the best idea is to tear down
the warehouse.

5 The developers need to choose between a contemporary
building style and a traditional one.

6 The building can't offer floor space for any stores.

7 Stores would have to be on the second floor.

8 Refurbishment would mean removing all the original
features of the building.

POST-LISTENING

Understanding figurative language

Figurative language refers to using words or expressions in a different way from their usual, literal meaning. For example, speakers may use comparisons or exaggerations instead of simple facts to make their point more interesting or dramatic. *The room was as cold as ice* is an example of figurative language and means that the room was very cold, although probably not literally freezing.

PRISM Digital Workbook

6 Match the figurative phrases in bold to their meanings.

1 I'm afraid we might be **biting off more than we can chew**. _____
2 I think it's a **potential goldmine**. _____
3 That building is more **like a prison** than a potential shopping mall. _____
4 We are going to give the old building **a new lease on life**. _____

a a fresh beginning
b trying to do a bigger job than we can realistically do
c a building that no one wants to visit
d an opportunity to make a lot of money

7 Which figurative phrases from Exercise 6 support knocking the old building down? Which support converting and modernizing it? Why?

Supports knocking the building down:

_____

_____

Supports converting and modernizing it:

_____

_____

8 Work with a partner. Use the figurative language from Exercise 6 to complete these sentences. Use your own ideas.

1 I bit off more than I could chew when I _____

_____

_____

2 _____ is a potential goldmine.
3 _____ seems like a prison.
4 I got a new lease on life when I _____

_____

_____

PRONUNCIATION FOR LISTENING

SKILLS

Emphasis in contrasting opinions

When you state an opinion that is different from somebody else's, you can emphasize your opinion by stressing the words or information that is different from theirs.

A: I think the original building has a lot of potential.

B: I think we really want to <u>transform</u> the area with something <u>modern</u>.

9 ▶ 5.2 Listen to the short conversations. Underline the words or phrases that speaker B stresses.

PRISM Digital Workbook

1 A: It has some beautiful original features.
   B: It looks like it's probably going to collapse!
2 A: Acquiring such an old building could be a huge mistake.
   B: Really? I think the project is going to be a great success.
3 A: It would be more of a transformation if we built a modern building made of materials like steel and glass.
   B: Couldn't we do both? We'll maintain more of a connection to the past if we include the old building as part of the new one.

10 Work with a partner. Practice saying the sentences in Exercise 9 with the underlined words stressed.

DISCUSSION

11 Work with a partner. Discuss the questions.

1 Do you think it is a good idea to add modern features to historical buildings? Why or why not?
2 Think of an old building that you are familiar with. Do you think it is better to tear it down, restore it to how it was originally, or add new features to it? Why?

⊙ LANGUAGE DEVELOPMENT

FUTURE FORMS

Will and *be going to* for predictions and expectations

You can use *will* and *be going to* to express predictions or to express an expectation.
This part of the city **will** look better after the old buildings are modernized.
A lot of people **are going to** move into the luxury apartments that are being built downtown.

You can use adverbs to show different degrees of certainty in predictions. Use *certainly*, *definitely*, *likely*, *possibly*, and *probably* after *will* or *be* in *be going to*. Use adverbs before *won't*. Use them before or after *be* in *be not going to*.
I'll definitely consider buying a house.
I **certainly won't** consider living in a city.
A lot of people **are probably going to** be interested in shopping in the new stores after they open.
We're probably **not going to** buy a home. / We probably **aren't going to** buy a home.

Use *maybe* and *perhaps* at the beginning of sentences.
Perhaps I **will** major in architecture so I can work to restore old buildings to their former glory.
Maybe I'll take an architecture class to learn more about building materials.

Use *be going to* for predictions when there is present evidence.
The building is old and has cracks in the bricks. It's **going to** collapse during the next earthquake.
There is no money in the budget to build a fountain. We're **not** / We **aren't going to** build it.

PRISM Digital Workbook

1 Complete the sentences by inserting the adverbs.

1 The building I want to move into was bought by a developer. It's going to be renovated before I move there. (certainly)

2 The construction team isn't going to begin work until next month. (probably)

3 The supporting walls are already up. The developers will complete the building soon. (likely)

4 The developer is drawing up his plans now. He will send me the apartment plans on Friday. (maybe)

5 I will help you with your architecture homework now. (definitely)

6 Joe is off from work on Friday. He will help you study for the architecture test. (perhaps)

2 Answer the questions about the future. Use *will/won't* or *be (not) going to* and adverbs to show certainty.

1 What kind of building will you live in five years from now?

_____

2 Do you think you will buy property? Why or why not?

_____

3 Do you think your classroom building will be around much longer? Why or why not?

_____

4 How do you think the buildings in this town or city will be different ten years from now?

_____

5 How do you think the downtown area will look ten years from now?

_____

ACADEMIC VOCABULARY FOR ARCHITECTURE AND TRANSFORMATION

3 Read the paragraph and write the verbs in bold next to the correct definitions.

PRISM Digital Workbook

ARCHITECTURE AND TRANSFORMATION

Architecture can **transform** the way people interact with the world, and architects must **anticipate** how a building will impact the local area. If the design of a building includes a lot of large windows, the people working inside **maintain** a connection with nature because they can see the sky. When people **abandon** old warehouses, which are left to collapse, this creates an opportunity for developers to **acquire** such properties and **convert** them into shops, apartments, and offices. Developing an old building can **contribute** to the improvement of a whole neighborhood, but suitable sites can be difficult to identify as cities **expand**.

1 _____ (v) to give something, especially money, to achieve something
2 _____ (v) to completely change the appearance, form, or character of something
3 _____ (v) to continue to have, or keep in existence
4 _____ (v) to increase in size, number, or importance
5 _____ (v) to expect that something will happen
6 _____ (v) to leave something forever
7 _____ (v) to change something from one thing to another
8 _____ (v) to buy or get something

4 Complete the sentences with the correct form of the verbs from Exercise 3.

1 We need to _____ the amount of retail space available.
2 We could _____ the local area with a new retail complex.
3 A new business district would _____ a lot to the local economy.
4 We _____ that the shopping area will bring $30 million in profit over the year.
5 The developer's plan to _____ a warehouse into an apartment building was a major success.
6 It may be difficult to _____ a piece of land within the city.
7 We can't _____ this project just because of a few setbacks.
8 We will _____ the number of houses in the new development, not increase it.

LISTENING 2

PREPARING TO LISTEN

UNDERSTANDING
KEY VOCABULARY

PRISM Digital Workbook

1 You are going to listen to a housing development meeting. Before you listen, read the sentences and write the words in bold next to the definitions.

1 We're **concerned** about the size of the building. Doesn't it look a bit too big for the area?
2 The old building is **adequate** and is in no danger of collapsing.
3 The **existing** decorations need to be changed completely to something more modern.
4 We need something that is **appropriate** for the local area.
5 The plan is very **sympathetic** to the local neighborhood and will leave the historical area as it is now.
6 A building of that size could be **controversial** because it is taller than all the others and might block everyone's view.
7 The plan is very **ambitious**; I'm not sure the developers will be able to finish on time.

a _____ (adj) that exists or is being used at the present time
b _____ (adj) causing a lot of disagreement or argument
c _____ (adj) enough or satisfactory for a specific purpose
d _____ (adj) showing support and agreement
e _____ (adj) not easily done or achieved
f _____ (adj) suitable or right for a specific situation or occasion
g _____ (adj) worried or anxious

2 Work with a partner. Use words from Exercise 1 to describe the pictures in Exercise 5 on page 114.

3 Work with a partner. Discuss possible solutions to the potential problems in the housing development plan.

USING YOUR KNOWLEDGE

problems	solutions
1 There will be a tall building blocking the light into another apartment building in the development.	
2 The modern design of the development doesn't fit in with the traditional buildings in the area.	
3 The natural area to build on is woodland, and residents want to keep it.	

WHILE LISTENING

4 ▶ 5.3 Listen to the housing development meeting. Use the T-chart in Exercise 3 to take notes on the solutions to the problems. Then compare your notes with a partner.

TAKING NOTES ON MAIN IDEAS

5 ▶ 5.3 Match the descriptions to the correct pictures. Then listen again to check your answers.

1 The proposed building site _____
2 The developers' proposal _____
3 The clients' preferred proposal _____
4 A proposal not discussed in the meeting _____

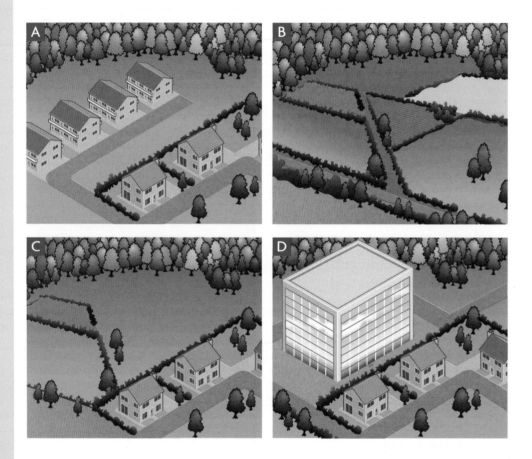

6 Who said the statements below? Write *D* (developers) or *C* (clients).

1 One of the biggest benefits of this plan is that it will create housing for as many as 200 people. _____
2 We could consider using reflective glass. _____
3 You described the natural area you'd like to build on as wasteland, but actually, those are woods. _____
4 As it stands, this plan ... would be very controversial. _____
5 What about more, smaller, shorter buildings? _____
6 Lots of glass is a great idea, but in my view the only viable option is to use brick. _____
7 How about we position the new buildings near the edge of the woods? _____
8 I feel confident we can come up with a good plan over the next two weeks. _____

POST-LISTENING

SKILLS

Understanding strong and tentative suggestions

When making suggestions, speakers use different language to emphasize their point, depending on how strongly they feel. To make a strong suggestion, speakers may use words like *only* or *strongly*. To make a tentative suggestion, speakers may use polite expressions like *We could* and *Wouldn't it be better if ...* . They may also state the suggestion as a question or use words like *maybe* or *probably*.

7 ▶ 5.4 Listen to the speakers. Are they making strong or tentative suggestions? Write *T* (tentative) or *S* (strong).

1 What about more smaller, shorter buildings? _____

2 In my view, the only viable option is to use brick. _____

3 This would probably be better with the existing houses. _____

4 I strongly recommend that you reconsider this. _____

5 Wouldn't it be better if we use the first design you supplied to identify a few priorities? _____

6 I like your thinking. I completely agree. _____

LISTENING FOR ATTITUDE

DISCUSSION

8 Work with a partner. Discuss the questions.

1 What do you think makes a house or apartment attractive?

2 Do you think it is better to live in an apartment or a house? Why?

3 Where do you think it is best to build new houses or developments: on old sites or in new green areas? Why?

4 Use your notes from Listening 1 and Listening 2 to answer the following questions. If you were designing an apartment building, where would you build it – in an old part of town or in a new part of town? How many people would live there? What features would it have?

SYNTHESIZING

SPEAKING

CRITICAL THINKING

At the end of this unit, you are going to do the Speaking Task below.

> Discuss the problem and possible solutions. An oil company owns an apartment building where 200 single workers and 50 families who work for the company live. The apartments are crowded, uncomfortable, and too far away from schools and the workers' main offices. The company needs the workers to move out of the current building one year from now. It has $3.8 million to spend on new accommodation projects.

ANALYZE

1 Work with a partner. In the table, list the problems mentioned in the Speaking Task. Then make a list of project requirements for the new apartment building.

problems	project requirements	solution A	solution B	solution C
crowded apartments	must have more space			

EVALUATE

2 Look at the three housing solutions on page 117. Compare your list of project requirements in Exercise 1 to each housing solution and answer the questions.

1 Which project requirements does each solution meet? Write ✔ in the table for solutions that meet each requirement.

2 Which project requirements does each solution not meet? Write ✘ in the table for those that don't meet the project requirements.

3 What would you need to change to make each solution fit the project requirements better?

Solution A: Colton Tower

- Available in six months
- Eight-story office building made of glass and steel
- Offices could be converted to bedrooms
- Bathrooms would be shared
- Shower rooms could be added on each floor
- Could accommodate up to 180 single workers and 40 families

- Located 1.8 miles (2.8 kilometers) from offices/factory
- Within walking distance of public schools or near bus lines for 4.9-mile (7.8-kilometer) trip to private school
- No facilities (parks, green spaces) for children nearby
- Price: $3.2 million
- Conversion cost: $600,000

Solution B: Avery House Hotel

- Available now
- 1920s hotel made of brick
- Could accommodate up to 210 single workers and 30 families
- Lots of traditional architectural features
- Hotel was abandoned 10 years ago

- Located 42.4 miles (68.2 kilometers) from offices/factory
- Located 6.2 miles (9.9 kilometers) from schools
- Plenty of open space for children to play and for adults to walk, ride bikes, etc.
- Price: $1.6 million
- Conversion cost: $2.4 million

Solution C: Land purchase

- Land available now
- Would need to complete government planning process before building (about 3 months; building would take another 3 months)
- Could accommodate up to 250 single people and 60 families in up to 6 apartment buildings, option to build more units in future

- Located 3.7 miles (5.9 kilometers) from offices/factory
- Located 7.4 miles (11.9 kilometers) from schools; accessible by car, bus, and train
- Plans could include full recreational facilities for adults and children
- Land price: $1.1 million
- Estimated building costs: $3 million

3 Work with another pair. Compare your responses to Exercise 2 and answer the questions.

1 Which solution do you think best meets the project requirements?

_____

_____

2 What points does each plan have that might impact your decision?

_____

_____

3 Can you reach a group decision? Why or why not?

_____

_____

PREPARATION FOR SPEAKING

PRONUNCIATION FOR SPEAKING

> **SKILLS**
>
> ### Emphasizing a word or idea to signal a problem
>
> Emphasizing or stressing a word in a sentence can help listeners understand its importance. Changing the emphasized or stressed word also changes the important piece of information in that sentence, and can be used to signal a problem.

PRISM Digital Workbook

1 ▶ 5.5 Listen. Underline the stressed word in each sentence. The first one is done for you.

1 The <u>main</u> issue is that most retailers don't want to do business here.
2 The main issue is that most retailers don't want to do business here.
3 The main issue is that most retailers don't want to do business here.
4 The main issue is that most retailers don't want to do business here.

2 Match the explanations with the sentences from Exercise 1.

a There are other types of business that will be happy to do business here, but retailers don't want to. _____
b There are other issues, but this is the most important one. _____
c Retailers are happy to put up advertising here, but they don't want to open shops in this area. _____
d There are aspects of the project that aren't issues, but this particular fact is a problem. _____

IDENTIFYING PROBLEMS AND SUGGESTING SOLUTIONS

> **SKILLS**
>
> ### Presenting a problem
>
> When presenting a problem, speakers often use phrases that signal there is an issue, such as *The problem is ...* , *The main issue is ...* , and *We need to find a way around ...* .

PRISM Digital Workbook

3 Put the words in order to make sentences.

1 of / prices / We / a / high / need / problem / to / the / find / around / way / .

_____

2 time / The / is / problem / enough / we / that / have / don't / .

_____

3 issue / main / The / is / people / that / our / don't / design / like / .

_____

4 a / around / way / find / need / We / to / problem / the / attracting / business / of / .

_____

5 the / is / building / The / issue / main / that / is / collapsing / .

_____

6 problem / that / The / is / no one / to / wants / area / in / live / the / .

_____

SKILLS

Making polite suggestions

Making a suggestion in the form of a question can be more polite than using a direct statement such as *I think ...* or *We have to ...* . This approach to making suggestions is more common when people are brainstorming and exploring a variety of ideas. Using it means the speaker is less likely to offend anyone. It is also a more formal way of speaking.

4 Write six suggestions using the structures in the box.

1 Could we ... 2 Can I suggest we ... 3 Should we consider ... 4 How about ... 5 Have you thought about ... 6 Why don't we ...	increase increasing	the budget?

5 Work with a partner. Take turns making suggestions for each of the problems. Use the structures from Exercise 4 to help you.

1 There is very little space for parking in the local area. (build parking lot)
   Could we build a parking lot?

2 The planned building is too high. (reduce height)

   _____

3 There isn't enough outdoor space. (turn the wasteland into a park)

   _____

4 There isn't any space for a garden around the apartment building. (build a rooftop garden)

   _____

5 The store units are too small to attract large retailers. (have more, larger units)

   _____

6 We won't be able to attract businesses to this area. (offer lower rents)

   _____

RESPONDING TO SUGGESTED SOLUTIONS

6 Read the responses. Does the speaker accept or reject the solution? Check (✔) the correct box.

	accept	reject
1 That's a great idea, but I'm not sure it addresses the problem.		
2 I like your thinking. I agree completely.		
3 I think that's a great idea.		
4 We thought that might be an option at first, but now we realize it won't work.		
5 That seems like an obvious solution, but it doesn't address the issue of cost.		
6 Let's do it.		

7 Work with a partner. Practice saying the sentences. Take turns making the suggestion and accepting or rejecting it, using phrases from Exercises 4 and 6.

1 How about building four smaller apartment buildings rather than one large one?
2 Should we include a community garden in the new development?
3 Can I suggest we reduce the size and scale of this development?

SPEAKING TASK

Discuss the problem and possible solutions. An oil company owns an apartment building where 200 single workers and 50 families who work for the company live. The apartments are crowded, uncomfortable, and too far away from schools and the workers' main offices. The company needs the workers to move out of the current building one year from now. It has $3.8 million to spend on new accommodation projects.

PREPARE

1 Work in groups of four. Look at the list of project requirements that you wrote in Critical Thinking. Choose one solution to the problem to look at.

2 Split into two pairs. One pair are the project developers. The other pair are the project clients.

> **Project developers:** You will present your solution to your clients. You need to highlight the positive aspects of your solution. Think about the negative aspects of your solution. What problems might the client identify? How could you respond?

> **Project clients:** You will listen to a presentation from the project developers. You need to ask questions about any information that they don't mention in their solution, or anything you aren't sure about. What problems might you need to identify?

3 In your pairs, look again at the table in Exercise 1 and the answers to the questions in Exercises 2 and 3 in Critical Thinking. Add any new information.

4 Refer to the Task Checklist below as you prepare for your discussion.

TASK CHECKLIST	✔
Identify problems and suggest solutions.	
Emphasize words and ideas to signal problems.	
Make polite suggestions.	
Respond to suggested solutions.	

PRACTICE

5 Practice your presentation/questions with your partner. Use your answers to Exercise 3 in Critical Thinking to help you.

DISCUSS

6 Discuss the problem and solution as a group.

ON CAMPUS

PREPARING TO LISTEN

SKILLS

At colleges and universities, you are expected to:

- plan your course of study
- manage your study time
- participate in class
- ask for help when necessary

1 You are going to listen to some university graduates discuss advice for students entering college. Work with a partner. Discuss what you think the graduates will say about each of the following topics:

_____ choosing classes

_____ participating in class

_____ making time to study

_____ relationships with teachers

WHILE LISTENING

2 ▶ 5.6 Listen and number the topics in Exercise 1 in the order you hear them.

3 ▶ 5.6 Listen again. Take notes in the table.

advice	reasons
1 Keep up with course work.	
2	
3	
4	

4 Work with a partner and compare your answers.

5 Work in small groups. Discuss the questions.

    1 Which piece of advice was most surprising to you?

    2 Do you agree with the advice? Why or why not?

PRACTICE

6 Match each piece of advice with a reason.

    1 Plan your schedule carefully. _____

    2 Read the class syllabus at the beginning of each class. _____

    3 Look at your notes before every class. _____

    4 Join a study group. _____

    5 Ask your teacher for help if necessary. _____

    a It will help you make connections between this class and the one before.

    b It's important to allow plenty of time for eating, sleeping, work, and study.

    c Teachers expect students to ask questions if they do not understand.

    d Talking about the material with other students will help you understand it.

    e It's important to know the class requirements.

7 Work in pairs. Think of two more pieces of advice for new students.
Give a reason for each one. Share your ideas with the class.

REAL-WORLD APPLICATION

8 Work in pairs. Look at the problems below. What advice could you give
to each person?

1 This class is really difficult, and I feel lost. It seems that everyone else in the class knows much more than I do.

2 It's difficult for me to speak out in class. Sometimes the teacher asks me a question and I can't think of the answer – even though I know it.

3 I'd like to take a class in astronomy, because it sounds interesting. But my friend says it's a difficult class, and I don't want to get a low grade.

4 I got sick in the middle of the semester, and now I've missed three classes. I'm worried that I've missed a lot of work. Should I drop the class?

5 I have plans to go away this weekend – but I just found out that I have a research paper due on Monday!

9 Work with a student from another pair. Choose one of the problems in
Exercise 8. Role-play a conversation between a student and an advisor.

10 Choose another problem and reverse roles.

LEARNING OBJECTIVES

Listening skills	Understand digressions; understand persuasive techniques
Pronunciation	Intonation related to emotion; use a neutral tone of voice
Speaking skill	Keep a discussion moving
Speaking Task	Participate in a discussion about an energy problem
On Campus	Work in groups

ACTIVATE YOUR KNOWLEDGE

Work with a partner. Discuss the questions.

1 How did people travel before cars were invented? What did people use to generate light and heat before electricity was discovered?

2 What fuel sources do we use for heat, light, and transportation today? What fuel sources do you think we will be using in 100 years?

3 Look at the photo. How does this neighborhood produce its energy? What other ways are there to produce energy?

PREPARING TO WATCH

1 Work with a partner. Discuss the questions.

1 What traditional fuel sources do we use for heat and light today?
2 What alternative fuel sources are used today?
3 What do you think will be our main source of power in 50 years? What about in 100 years?

2 Look at the pictures from the video. Discuss the questions with a partner.

1 Do you think these homes use a lot of energy? Why or why not?
2 What are the benefits of putting solar panels on a home?
3 In what parts of the world do you think solar panels are the most beneficial? Why?

GLOSSARY

mind-blowing (adj) surprising, shocking, and often difficult to understand or imagine

shrink (v) to become smaller or cause something to become smaller

solar panel (n) a flat device that changes energy from the sun into electricity

electric meter (n) a device that measures the amount of electricity used

kilowatt (n) a unit for measuring electrical power (1 kilowatt = 1000 watts)

WHILE WATCHING

3 ▶ Watch the video. Write *T* (true) or *F* (false) next to the statements. Correct the false statements.

_____ 1 The Mathis family lives in an energy-efficient home.

_____ 2 Their electric bills have been slightly reduced because of the solar panels on the roof.

_____ 3 Solar panels can reduce a home's energy consumption by 60%.

_____ 4 According to John Rawlston, solar homes can consume less than zero kilowatts of electricity.

_____ 5 Mr. and Mrs. Mathis check their meter every day.

4 ▶ Watch again. For each main idea, write a supporting detail.

1 Solar panels resulted in savings for the Mathis family.

_____

2 John Rawlston builds homes in California and has helped homeowners reduce their energy usage.

_____

3 California builders hope to expand the use of solar panels outside their state.

_____

5 Work with a partner and discuss the questions.

1 Which is probably more important to the Mathis family, saving money or helping the environment? Why?

2 The speaker states that solar panels will be usable in places with less light soon. Do you think the panels will be as efficient in those places? Why or why not?

3 What could governments do to encourage homeowners to install solar panels?

DISCUSSION

6 Discuss the questions with your partner. Compare your answers with another pair.

1 Are solar panels commonly used on buildings in your neighborhood?

2 Would you use solar energy in your home? Why or why not?

3 What other alternative energy sources are used in your city or country?

UNDERSTANDING MAIN IDEAS

UNDERSTANDING DETAILS

MAKING INFERENCES

LISTENING

LISTENING 1

PREPARING TO LISTEN

UNDERSTANDING KEY VOCABULARY

1 You are going to listen to a radio interview about the island of El Hierro in Spain. Before you listen, read the definitions. Complete the sentences with the correct form of the words in bold.

> **capacity** (n) the amount that something can produce
> **consistent** (adj) always acting in a similar way
> **cycle** (n) a set of events that repeat themselves regularly in the same order
> **element** (n) one part of something
> **generate** (v) to produce
> **mainland** (n) the biggest or primary part of a country, not including the islands around it
> **network** (n) a group formed by connected parts
> **reservoir** (n) a lake that stores and supplies water

1 A solar panel is one _____ needed to make the office more energy efficient. Another is special lightbulbs.
2 The president has a _____ voting record; he always supports alternative energy sources.
3 The _____ stores enough water to supply the entire town for a year.
4 The island mainly has gasoline-powered cars, but the _____ has more electric cars.
5 The engineer set the batteries to recharge on a 24-hour _____ .
6 The _____ allows all the computers in the office to communicate with each other.
7 The temperature needs to be higher in order to _____ enough heat to warm the building.
8 The wind turbines are operating at full _____ and should be able to produce electricity for the entire city.

2 Before you listen to the radio interview, complete the fact file with the words from the box.

area   government   mainland   population

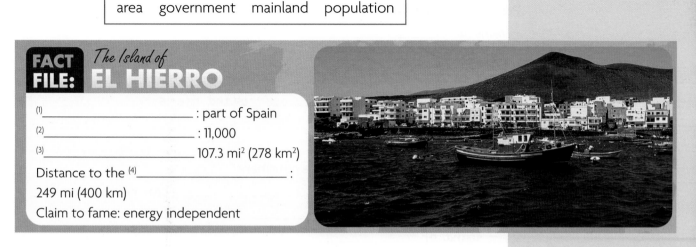

FACT FILE: *The Island of* **EL HIERRO**

(1)_____ : part of Spain
(2)_____ : 11,000
(3)_____ 107.3 mi² (278 km²)
Distance to the (4)_____ :
249 mi (400 km)
Claim to fame: energy independent

3 Work in pairs. Answer the questions.

1 What do you think life is like on El Hierro?
2 What would probably need to be imported from the mainland?
3 What sort of energy supply do you think is available there?
4 What do you think *energy independent* means?

WHILE LISTENING

4 ▶ 6.1 Listen to the radio interview about El Hierro. Choose the ending for each sentence.

1 The people of El Hierro ...
   a need to buy all of their oil.
   b need to buy 30% of their oil.
   c don't need to buy any oil.
2 El Hierro's energy is provided by ...
   a wind and hydroelectric power.
   b solar and wind power and imported oil.
   c solar and hydroelectric power.
3 The system also provides water for ...
   a a small lake filled with fish.
   b a water park.
   c drinking and agriculture.

5 ▶ 6.2 Listen to the first part of the radio interview again. Complete the student's notes about Pedro Rodriguez with the missing details.

<u>Pedro Rodriguez</u>
– owns a (1)_____
– has lived there (2)_____
– lived in (3)_____ for most of his life
– city life is (4)_____ ; island life is
(5)_____

<u>What's great about El Hierro</u>
– in the city, everyone hurries everywhere
– you are surrounded by (6)_____ , can never relax
– career was in (7)_____
  – sound of (8)_____
  – peace and (9)_____
– energy (10)_____
– before, power came from (11)_____
  – shipped (12)_____ barrels from the
(13)_____ every year
  – cost (14)_____ a year

6 ▶ 6.3 Now listen to the second part of the radio interview again. Complete the student's notes about wind and hydroelectric power with the missing details.

<u>Wind Power</u>
– wind blows (1)_____ hours a year
  – (2)_____ % of the year
– generate energy by using (3)_____
  – capacity of (4)_____ megawatts
  – enough to power (5)_____ homes
<u>Hydroelectric power</u>
– when energy of moving (6)_____ is converted
into electricity
  – usually from a river with a (7)_____
  – theirs is from a reservoir inside a (8)_____
  – reservoir holds (9)_____ cubic feet
  – is (10)_____ feet above (11)_____

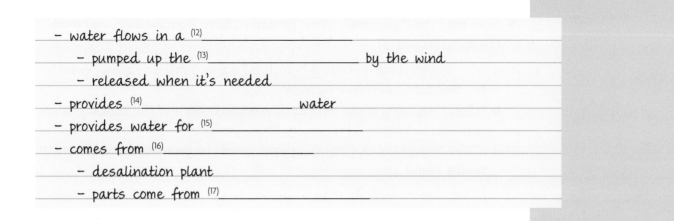

– water flows in a (12)_____
  – pumped up the (13)_____ by the wind
  – released when it's needed
– provides (14)_____ water
– provides water for (15)_____
– comes from (16)_____
  – desalination plant
  – parts come from (17)_____

POST-LISTENING

Understanding digressions

Speakers sometimes digress (move away from) the main topic in a conversation. Often they do this because they haven't prepared answers to or aren't thinking about the question they have been asked. Recognizing when someone is digressing can help you move the focus back to the main topic of a conversation.

7 Read the topics Pedro talks about during the interview. Write *MT* (main topic) or *D* (digression).

1 Peace and quiet _____
2 Traffic in Madrid _____
3 The fast pace of city life _____
4 The sound of the sea _____
5 The banking profession _____
6 Freedom on the island _____

8 Match the questions with relevant answers. Then check your answers with a partner.

1 What is the most important power source on El Hierro? _____
2 Can life be hard on El Hierro? _____
3 What do you miss about living on the mainland? _____

Answers

a Having easy access to facilities, like movie theaters and a variety of restaurants.
b Probably the wind turbines. Without them we wouldn't be able to power the pump system for the water.
c It can be difficult in the winter, when the sea is rough. Basic supplies often take several days longer to arrive.

LISTENING FOR TEXT ORGANIZATION

PRISM Digital Workbook

9 Now read the digressions. What questions from Exercise 8 do you think the speakers heard?

a My children think it's boring here, but I wanted them to grow up with the freedom to explore outside. _____

b I didn't like living in my old city. It was too noisy and the buildings were too tall. _____

c We've thought about installing solar panels to generate extra electricity on the island. _____

PRONUNCIATION FOR LISTENING

SKILLS

Intonation related to emotion

Intonation is the rise and fall of pitch in a person's voice. Intonation can tell you how a speaker feels at that moment or about the topic. Intonation can convey a variety of emotions – for example, annoyance, sadness, surprise, or excitement.

PRISM Digital Workbook

10 ▶ 6.4 Listen to the same sentence spoken with four different emotions. Then practice saying them with a partner.

Max went to Spain.

1 annoyance   3 surprise
2 sadness   4 excitement

11 ▶ 6.5 Listen to the sentences. Write the emotion expressed in the sentences. Use the words from Exercise 10.

1 Don't you like it here? _____
2 El Hierro is completely energy independent. _____
3 Well, if you've spent a day or two here, you may have noticed we have a lot of wind. _____
4 But doesn't hydroelectric power require a river and a dam? _____
5 In fact, I've just come from the desalination plant where we're having some problems today. _____

12 Work with a partner. Take turns saying the sentences with different emotions. Can your partner guess which emotion you're expressing?

DISCUSSION

13 Work with a partner. Discuss the questions.

1 What alternatives to fossil fuels are you familiar with? What are their advantages and disadvantages?
2 What kinds of energy would work best in your community? Explain.

CONNECTING IDEAS BETWEEN SENTENCES

Transition words and phrases

Remember, you can connect ideas using transition words and phrases to show different relationships between sentences, such as giving extra information, comparing and contrasting, and explaining a result.

We're a long way from the mainland, **so** delivery of anything takes at least a few days. (explaining a result)

Yes, that's right. **What's more,** the system also provides our drinking water and water for use in agriculture. (giving extra information)

It's a real challenge living here. **On the other hand,** we all love it. (comparing and contrasting)

1 Complete the tables with the transition words and phrases from the box.

| and as a result   Moreover,   Furthermore,   In addition, |
| Even so,   Nevertheless,   therefore |

giving extra information		
Yes, that's right.	What's more, _____ _____	the system also provides our drinking water and water for use in agriculture.

comparing and contrasting		
Well, it's a real challenge living here.	On the other hand, _____ _____	we all love it.

explaining a result		
We're a long way from the mainland,	so _____ _____	delivery of anything takes a few days.

2 Work in pairs. Use the words and phrases from the middle columns in Exercise 1 to connect the sentences.

1 City life is stressful. Island life is relaxing. (comparing and contrasting)

_____

2 The houses use solar energy. They have water-recycling systems. (giving extra information)

_____

3 Dams can damage habitats. They have to be planned carefully. (explaining a result)

_____

4 The wind blows for 30% of the year. That isn't enough to provide all of the island's electricity. (comparing and contrasting)

_____

5 This electric car can go just over 62 miles per hour. The battery can be charged using solar power. (giving extra information)

_____

6 The system requires that water moves from a high place to a lower place. We've placed a water tank on a hill. (explaining a result)

_____

THE PASSIVE VOICE

LANGUAGE

Use the passive voice when the result of an action is more important than who or what made it happen (the agent). Form the passive voice using the auxiliary verb *be* + the past participle. *Be* must agree with the subject.

Hydroelectric power is when the energy of moving water **is converted** into another form. (Note: It is not important to know who or what converts the energy.)
Different machines **are used** to convert the energy.

Speakers usually omit the agent when they talk about a process or to report news events. The listener needs to focus on the action and not who performed the action.

However, use a *by* + agent phrase if the agent is important or if the meaning of the sentence would be unclear without it.
The water **is pumped** up the hill <u>by the wind</u>.

When using modals with the passive voice, use a modal + *be* + past participle of the main verb. *Not* comes after the modal in the negative form.
Hydroelectric power **can be used** as a cheap alternative to fossil fuels.
Nuclear power **should not be used** in countries where it has been banned.

3 ► 6.6 Listen to each statement. Write *A* (active) or *P* (passive). Then compare your answers with a partner.

1 _____ 3 _____ 5 _____
2 _____ 4 _____ 6 _____

4 Complete the paragraph below using the passive voice.

Geothermal energy (1)_____ (use) in many countries around the world because it is one of the few truly renewable energy sources. It (2)_____ (create) by the heat from the Earth. The main sources of this heat can range from the shallow ground to the hot water and hot rock that (3)_____ (find) beneath the surface of the Earth. This energy can also (4)_____ (extract) even deeper below the Earth's surface, where extremely hot temperatures (5)_____ (cause) by magma and molten rock. In many locations around the world, wells (6)_____ (drill) into underground reservoirs in order to generate electricity. At some power plants, power (7)_____ (supply) by steam from a water-powered generator. Hot water near the surface of the Earth (8)_____ (can / use) to provide heat for buildings, for growing plants in greenhouses, drying crops, heating water at fish farms, and pasteurizing milk.

ACADEMIC VOCABULARY FOR NETWORKS AND SYSTEMS

5 Read the article. Write the words in bold next to the definitions.

With the steady **decline** in supplies of coal and oil, exploring the **potential** of alternative energy sources has increased in recent decades. Installing an alternative energy **generation** system to power an entire town is a huge **challenge**. A single energy **source**, such as solar or wind power, rarely has the **capacity** to do this. Engineers and designers therefore need to come up with a **network** of technologies to provide a consistent power supply from a variety of sources. Each **element** of the system must take advantage of a natural resource when it is available. Wind turbines need a certain amount of wind to produce electricity, so when the wind slows or stops, another part of the system needs to be able to perform the same task.

1 _____ (n) the production of energy in a particular form
2 _____ (n) part of something
3 _____ (n) in this context, the ability to do something
4 _____ (n) the origin or place something comes from
5 _____ (n) something requiring great effort to do successfully
6 _____ (n) a system of parts that work together
7 _____ (n) ability for something to develop, achieve, or succeed
8 _____ (n) a gradual decrease in something

PREPARING TO LISTEN

1 You are going to listen to a meeting about saving energy in an office. Before you listen, look at the picture and discuss the questions with a partner.

1 What things in an office environment use energy?
2 How could energy be saved in an office environment?

2 Read the text. Write the correct form of the words in bold next to the definitions.

Simple measures to reduce energy **consumption** can cut office energy bills by up to 20%, such as reducing the **volume** of trash. Some businesses, however, are going further to be environmentally friendly. The **function** of large energy-saving plans is to save a lot of money as well as the environment, but there are **limitations**. One **drawback** of making an office more **efficient** is that it is expensive in the beginning, although money is saved over time. Large, complex, energy-saving projects can also have a **maintenance** cost that often isn't factored in, which can be expensive, especially when the new technology is still **experimental**.

PRISM Digital Workbook

1 _____ (n) the act of using, eating, or drinking something
2 _____ (n) the work needed to keep something in good condition
3 _____ (adj) new and not tested
4 _____ (adj) producing good results without waste
5 _____ (n) a situation that restricts something
6 _____ (n) a role or purpose
7 _____ (n) the number or amount of something
8 _____ (n) a disadvantage or negative part of a situation

WHILE LISTENING

3 ▶ 6.7 Listen to a meeting about saving energy at an office. Complete the notes on the speakers' proposed solutions to the office energy problem. Check (✔) the ideas that the speakers identify as "large-scale."

speaker	proposed solutions	large-scale
Zara	Install (1)_____ on the roof	
Allen	Change to (2)_____ lightbulbs	
Abdul	Clean dirty windows to get more (3)_____	
	Turn off (4)_____ when get up from desk	
Zara	Turn off (5)_____ when it isn't hot	
	Get rid of one (6)_____	
	Install a solar (7)_____ heating system	

4 ▶ 6.7 Listen to the meeting again. Complete the sentences with the words or phrases you hear.

1 One alternative energy source is to install _____ on the roof.
2 Energy-efficient lightbulbs pay for themselves _____ .
3 _____ the windows will let more natural light in.
4 They don't really need _____ photocopiers.
5 They could also turn off computer screens and _____ .
6 Some systems are technically complex. There's also the problem of _____ , and they would need to pay a technician to make repairs.
7 They could market themselves as a _____ business.
8 They want to immediately start making _____ changes and look into more complex changes later.

SKILLS

Understanding persuasive techniques

When giving an opinion or a suggestion in a discussion, speakers often use persuasive language to try to convince listeners that they are right, that their suggestions are good ideas, or that there is a problem with someone else's idea. Here are examples of sentences that use different persuasive techniques:

I see your point. Even so, I think solar panels are the best idea. (challenging a point)
Don't you think that solar panels are a good idea? (asking a question)
Trust me when I say that solar panels are the best idea. (reassuring)
You also need to consider the cost of solar panels. (adding information)
By and large, I see what you're saying, but solar panels are just more efficient. (expressing reservations)

5 Match the persuasive techniques to the sentences from the meeting.

1 Well, if we really want to do something to save on electricity costs long-term, why don't we consider an alternative energy source? _____

2 No, I really like that idea because once it's installed, the system will have a low operating cost, and it's an environmentally friendly way to generate electricity, which are two big positive points, but there are other considerations. For example, we'd have to look at the generating capacity of the system. _____

3 The fact is, both systems Zara mentioned are technically complex and expensive to install. _____

4 I can't help but feel that a solar energy project would be too ambitious. _____

5 I can assure you that the company wouldn't do anything unsafe or illegal. _____

a challenging a point
b asking a question
c reassuring
d adding information
e expressing reservations

6 Work with a partner. Match the sentences to the persuasive techniques in Exercise 5.

1 On that point, we could employ a window cleaner at a relatively low cost. _____

2 I don't think we need to worry about the cost of installing a system until we find one that would work for us. _____

3 I'm not convinced that we get enough sunshine here to make a solar power system effective. _____

4 Have you thought more about my idea of getting rid of a photocopier? _____

5 I see what you mean, but consider the fact that sometimes we do need to leave our computer screens on. _____

DISCUSSION

SYNTHESIZING

7 Work with a partner. Discuss the questions.

1 What other reasons can you think of for using alternative energy sources at home or in the workplace?

2 Can you think of ways to reduce energy consumption at home?

3 Use your notes from Listening 1 and Listening 2 to answer the following questions. Would it be possible to make your home more energy efficient like El Hierro or the office you heard about in Listening 2? If so, what ideas would be appropriate? If not, why not?

SPEAKING

CRITICAL THINKING

At the end of this unit, you are going to do the Speaking Task below.

> How can we save energy in our college/university?

▲ REMEMBER

1 Work with a partner. Look back at your notes from Listening 2, Exercise 3. What solutions were proposed in the meeting? What were the large-scale solutions?

▲ ANALYZE

2 With your partner, brainstorm some possible problems with energy use at a college or university. Think of as many as you can. Make a list.

lights left on at night

_____

_____

_____

_____

_____

▲ EVALUATE

3 Choose the three biggest problems and write them at the top of the table.

problems	1	2	3
possible solutions			

4 Think of possible solutions to each problem and add them to the table. Include at least two large-scale solutions (alternative sources of energy) and at least two small-scale solutions (ways of reducing consumption) for each problem. You will use this table again for the Speaking Task at the end of this unit.

PREPARATION FOR SPEAKING

KEEPING A DISCUSSION MOVING

Asking for input, summarizing, and keeping a discussion moving

In some discussions, such as meetings in a committee or in an office, someone usually leads the discussion points. The leader usually asks participants to provide input on the discussion, summarizes main points, and keeps the discussion moving. There are certain words and phrases a leader might use to ask for input, summarize, or keep a discussion moving.

asking for input
What do you think?
Does anyone have anything to add?

keeping a discussion moving
We'd better move on to the next point.
Let's finish this point and then move on.

summarizing
To summarize the key points ...
Do we all agree that ... ?

PRISM **Digital** Workbook

1   Match the speaker's sentences to the functions.

1   Sorry, but that's not really what we're discussing right now. _____
2   Does anyone have anything to say about this idea? _____
3   I'd just like to recap the key points so far. _____

a   asking for input
b   keeping the discussion moving / on topic
c   summarizing

2   Complete the conversation with the expressions from the box.

> a   Does anyone have anything to say
> b   Sorry, but that's really not what we're
> c   To summarize the key points

A: So, (1)_____ : we agree that we want to reduce energy consumption, and we want to consider an alternative energy source. (2)_____ about a solar energy system?

B: I'm more concerned about our water usage.

C: (3)_____ discussing right now.

3   ▶ 6.8   Listen and check your answers.

Dealing with interruptions and digressions

During a discussion, participants sometimes need to deal with interruptions or digressions from the topic. When speaking firmly to someone, you can still be polite by beginning phrases with *Sorry, but ...* or *Excuse me, but ...* and using expressions such as *Could you possibly ...* and *Would you mind ...* For example:

Excuse me, but I'd just like to finish this point.
Sorry, but if you give me one more minute, I'm about to finish.
Could you possibly give me one more minute?
Would you mind if I finish this last point?

PRISM Digital Workbook

4 Work with a partner and practice making the sentences more polite.

1 Wait. I haven't finished speaking.
2 I don't understand. Explain.
3 That's off the topic.
4 Stop talking. We can't hear what Tom is saying.

PRONUNCIATION FOR SPEAKING

Using a neutral tone of voice

When you feel excited, upset, or angry, your tone of voice can sound argumentative. Maintaining a neutral, relaxed tone of voice can help stop a request for clarification on a point from sounding like a challenge or argument.

PRISM Digital Workbook

5 ▶ 6.9 Listen to the sentences. How does the speaker sound? Write *A* (argumentative) or *N* (neutral).

1 Sorry, but could you hold that thought until Abdul has finished, please? __A__
2 Sorry, but could you hold that thought until Abdul has finished, please? __N__
3 So are you saying you're against using solar power? _____
4 Could I just clarify something here? Are we talking about solar power or wind power? _____
5 Do you mean this is completely new technology? _____
6 Could I just clarify something here? Could we even use a solar power system on the roof of the building? _____

6 Work with a partner. Take turns saying the sentences in Exercise 5. Use either a neutral or an argumentative tone. Can your partner guess which tone you're using?

SPEAKING TASK

How can we save energy in our college/university?

Work in groups of three or four. Have a meeting using the agenda below. Each student should lead the discussion for one item on the agenda.

AGENDA
1 Current problems with energy consumption
2 Possible alternative sources of energy (large-scale ideas)
3 Other ways of reducing consumption (small-scale ideas)
4 Summary and conclusions

PREPARE

1 Discuss the main problems with energy consumption in your college/ university. Review the table of problems and possible solutions you created in Exercise 3 in Critical Thinking. Add any new ideas.

2 Each member of the group picks two or three ideas to raise for each agenda point in the discussion. Work on your own and make notes on the language you might use to raise your point.

3 Make notes on language that you might use to keep the discussion on topic.

4 Refer to the Task Checklist below as you prepare for your discussion.

TASK CHECKLIST	✔
Ask for opinions on the topic.	
Use a neutral tone of voice.	
Clarify information.	
Deal with interruptions and digressions from the topic.	
Summarize what's already been discussed.	

DISCUSS

5 Have the discussion. Take turns leading the discussion.

6 Did you come to any conclusions at the end? Why or why not?

WORKING IN GROUPS

PREPARING TO LISTEN

1 Work in small groups. Discuss the questions.

1 Why do teachers often assign group projects to students?
2 What are the advantages of working in groups?
3 What can go wrong when people work in groups?

WHILE LISTENING

2 ▶ 6.10 Listen to the excerpt from a psychology lecture about group work. Circle the main point.

a Employers value employees who can work well with others.
b There are advantages and disadvantages to working in groups.
c There are ways to ensure that groups work well.

3 ▶ 6.10 Listen to the excerpt again. Answer the questions.

1 What skill is important to employers nowadays?
2 What does "working well with other people" involve?
3 Why do groups sometimes fail to meet their goals?
4 What are two ways to help groups succeed?
5 How do many groups assign roles to group members?
6 What examples of roles are mentioned?

4 Work with a partner and compare your answers. Listen again if necessary. Do you agree with the speaker's suggestions?

SKILLS

Suggestions for working in groups

- Divide the work into stages
- Agree on a clear timeline
- Assign a role to each member of the group

PRACTICE

5 Here are some common roles for participants in group projects. Match the roles with the descriptions.

chairperson   communicator   group leader
reporter   recorder   technical expert

1 _____	2 _____	3 _____
helps group members with computer or software problems; collects and records data	collects contact information; contacts group members about meetings and important deadlines	records decisions made and which group members will do each task

4 _____	5 _____	6 _____
reports back to class or professor; summarizes the group's progress and/or conclusions	schedules meetings; prepares the agenda for the meeting; distributes work	chairs meetings (keeps the discussion moving); asks for input from group members

6 Work in small groups. Discuss the questions.

1 Here are some other possible roles for group members. What do you think these roles involve?

language expert   timekeeper   harmonizer   information gatherer

2 Can you think of any other useful roles?
3 Which roles are the most important?
4 Which role(s) would you prefer? Why?

REAL-WORLD APPLICATION

7 Work in groups of 4–6. Read the following assignment. Discuss the questions.

Prepare a presentation on energy use and practical, cost-effective ways for local businesses to save water. You will present the information to the city council two weeks from today.

1 What information do you need to find out? How will you do that?
2 What stages are involved in the project? Work out a timeline.
3 What roles will you assign? What will each person do?

8 Report your plan to the class.

LEARNING OBJECTIVES

Listening skills	Infer opinions; distinguish fact from opinion
Pronunciation	Stress in word families; stress in hedging language
Speaking skill	Language for debates
Speaking Task	Have an informal debate
On Campus	Choose a major

ART AND DESIGN

ACTIVATE YOUR KNOWLEDGE

Work with a partner. Discuss the questions.

1 Do you think the sculpture in this photo is art? Why or why not?

2 What do you think makes something art?

3 What kind of art is popular in your country? What kind of art do you like?

WATCH AND LISTEN

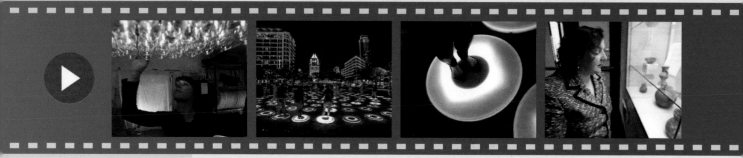

PREPARING TO WATCH

ACTIVATING YOUR KNOWLEDGE

1 Work with a partner. Discuss the questions.

1 Who are some famous artists you are familiar with?
2 What kind of art do they create?
3 What are their most famous works of art?
4 How do you define art?

PREDICTING CONTENT USING VISUALS

2 Look at the pictures from the video. For each picture, write two adjectives in the table to describe the art.

picture	adjectives
1	
2	
3	
4	

GLOSSARY

charcoal (n) a hard, black substance similar to coal that can be used as fuel or to draw with

perspective (n) the way you think about something

artwork (n) an object made by an artist, such as a picture or statue

swirl (n) a twisting, circular shape

elusive (adj) difficult to describe, find, achieve, or remember

perceive (v) to think of something in a particular way

WHILE WATCHING

3 ▶ Watch the video. Circle the correct answer.

UNDERSTANDING MAIN IDEAS

1 Which best describes Jen Lewin's artistic style?
   a traditional
   b interactive new media
   c new media

2 Which of the following is not a characteristic of her work?
   a computer generated
   b combination of old and new
   c charcoal drawn

3 Why is this style of art successful?
   a It connects groups of people and brings them together.
   b Children love interacting with artworks.
   c It combines construction and art.

4 ▶ Watch again. Use the words from the box to complete the summary.

SUMMARIZING

encourage	light up	networked	perspective

Jen Lewin is a different kind of artist. She uses computers and computer data to create colorful art. From her (1)_____ , what she does is no different than using paint on a canvas. Her pieces include sound and light to (2)_____ viewers to move around and activate parts of the artwork. Certain works can be jumped on, (3)_____ , and send video messages. It is no surprise that interactive works of art are so successful today. Just like the Internet, this kind of art brings people together in a more (4)_____ , connected way.

5 Write each phrase from the box in the correct column of the table.

MAKING INFERENCES

allows the viewer only to reflect   allows the viewer to reflect and interact
uses paint and other similar materials   uses new technologies

new media art	traditional art
1 _____	3 _____
2 _____	4 _____

DISCUSSION

6 Work with a partner. Discuss the questions.

1 Would you go to an exhibit featuring Jen Lewin's work? Why or why not?
2 What is appealing about her art? Have you seen other artworks like hers?
3 Do you prefer traditional art, or more modern interactive works? Why?

LISTENING

LISTENING 1

PREPARING TO LISTEN

1 You are going to listen to a radio report about the work of a graffiti artist. Before you listen, read the sentences and write the words in bold next to the definitions.

1 People in the community want to **remove** graffiti from their buildings. They want to make the neighborhood a more beautiful, friendlier place to live.

2 The artist sees his paintings as a form of **self-expression**. He shows a different part of his personality in every painting.

3 Many artists carefully consider the **composition** of their paintings, especially where people are placed in relation to other objects.

4 The newspaper review contained a lot of **criticism** about the artist's work.

5 Police officers discovered the **identity** of the graffiti artist when he was caught on camera painting on an office building.

6 The critic will **comment** on the new paintings in the museum when he writes about them in his next article.

7 Some people believe that all artists have the **right** to paint wherever they want without being punished.

8 The unusual colors and shapes in the painting showed the artist's **creativity**.

a _____ (n) who someone is; the qualities that make a person different from others

b _____ (n) a person's opportunity to act and be treated in particular ways that the law promises to protect for the benefit of society

c _____ (v) to take something away from an object, group, or place

d _____ (n) how someone expresses their personality, emotions, or ideas, especially through art, music, or acting

e _____ (v) to express an opinion

f _____ (n) the way that people or things are arranged in a painting or photograph

g _____ (n) the ability to produce original and unusual ideas, or to make something new or imaginative

h _____ (n) the act of giving your opinion or judgment about the good or bad qualities of something or someone, especially books, films, etc.

2 Look at the photo. Discuss the questions in pairs.

1 Describe the image. Where do you think it might be found?
2 Who do you think might have painted it? Why?

graffiti

PREDICTING CONTENT USING VISUALS

WHILE LISTENING

3 ▶ 7.1 Listen to the radio report. Then answer the questions.

1 Where is this piece of graffiti?
   a at an art museum
   b on a person's house
   c on an office building
2 What is the host trying to learn?
   a people's opinion about the graffiti
   b if graffiti is art or a crime
   c what the laws are regarding graffiti
3 Do these people who are interviewed like the graffiti? Circle *yes* or *no*.
   a Alex   yes   no
   b office worker   yes   no
   c police officer   yes   no
   d Simone   yes   no
   e Joseph   yes   no

LISTENING FOR MAIN IDEAS

4 ▶ 7.1 Listen again. Complete the table with the different opinions of each person interviewed.

TAKING NOTES ON OPINION

person	opinions
Alex	
office worker	
police officer	
Simone	
Joseph	

POST-LISTENING

5 Use your notes from Exercise 4 to match the speakers to their statements. Then compare answers with a partner.

1 Alex   3 police officer   5 Joseph
2 office worker   4 Simone

a We remove all graffiti because it's the law. _____
b I don't really like it. It's just graffiti, isn't it? _____
c I just think it's cool – it has a distinctive style. _____
d The people who own this building didn't ask for this, did they? _____
e I think he or she could make a lot of money. _____
f It's something interesting to look at, and it looks good, doesn't it? _____
g I think this type of art is a really good way of expressing your ideas. _____
h The artist is communicating a message about how young people feel. _____
i The color scheme and the composition work very well together. _____
j I actually really like it, despite the fact that it's illegal. _____

Inferring opinions

Sometimes when people speak, they try to sound neutral or conceal their opinion about a topic, usually to appear fair and professional. However, the words and phrases used can often reveal different, more personal opinions.

MAKING INFERENCES

6 Look at the words each person used to describe the graffiti painter and the graffiti. Answer the questions.

police officer	the artist, very creative, a piece of art, artistic, expressive, artwork, vandalism
host	the area's mystery graffiti artist, our illegal painter, this piece of vandalism

PRISM **Digital** Workbook

1 Which words and phrases in the table have positive connotations?
2 Which words and phrases have negative connotations?
3 Which person do you think likes the painting more? Does this surprise you? Explain.

PRONUNCIATION FOR LISTENING

Stress in word families

Changing the form of a word sometimes changes the stress, too. Say the stressed syllable in a longer, louder way than the other syllables. The stressed syllables in these words are underlined.

ap-ply (v)   ap-pli-ca-tion (n)

7 ▶ **7.2** Listen and underline the stressed syllable in each word. The first two are underlined for you.

verb	noun
1 <u>de</u>-co-rate	de-co-<u>ra</u>-tion
2 com-<u>pose</u>	com-po-<u>si</u>-tion
3 com-mu-ni-cate	com-mu-ni-ca-tion
4 cre-ate	cre-a-tion
5 ex-hib-it	ex-hi-bi-tion
6 re-com-mend	re-com-men-da-tion

noun	adjective
7 ac-tiv-i-ty	ac-tive
8 ar-tist	ar-tis-tic

8 Work with a partner. Practice reading the word pairs from Exercise 7 with the correct stress.

DISCUSSION

9 Work with a partner. Discuss the questions.

1 Is there street art in your town or city? If so, what do you think of it?
2 Would you like to have street art outside your home? Why or why not?
3 Do you think street art and graffiti should be illegal? Why or why not?

⊙ LANGUAGE DEVELOPMENT

RELATIVE CLAUSES

Relative clauses (also called *adjective clauses*) add information about nouns. They begin with the relative pronouns *who, that, which, whose, where,* or *when*. In the example, the relative pronoun *who* introduces more information about the subject.

The person ↰ **who painted the graffiti** is very creative.

Use *who* or *that* for people. Use *where* for places.

Use *which* or *that* for things or ideas. Use *whose* for possession.

Use *when* for time.

A relative clause must include a verb.

Identifying and nonidentifying relative clauses

Identifying relative clauses give *essential* information about the nouns they describe. This information often identifies or distinguishes the noun.

Art **that is painted on city buildings** *is called graffiti.* (The information identifies a particular type of art – not all types of art.)

My *sister* **who lives in San Francisco** *loves street art.* (The information distinguishes this sister from others; it implies there is more than one sister.)

Nonidentifying relative clauses give *extra, nonessential* information about the nouns they describe. In writing, use commas before and after the clause. In speaking, use a short pause before and after the clause.

Graffiti, **which is often painted on city buildings without permission,** *is a big topic of debate right now.* (The information does not identify the type of graffiti; it gives more information about it.)

My *sister,* **who lives in San Francisco,** *loves street art.* (The information is extra, not essential; it also implies the speaker has only one sister.)

Nonidentifying relative clauses are more common in formal speaking than in informal speaking.

PRISM **Digital** Workbook

1 Complete the sentences with the correct relative pronoun in parentheses. Underline the noun that each relative clause refers to.

1 Ray Noland, _____ is better known as "CRO," is a well-known street artist in Chicago. (who / whose / which)

2 The people _____ houses are covered in graffiti are worried about their property values. (who / whose / where)

3 The museum _____ the *Mona Lisa* is located is in Paris, France. (that / which / where)

4 It is sometimes better to visit museums on Mondays _____ fewer tourists are there. (that / where / when)

2 Read the sentences. Underline the relative clauses and write *I* (identifying) or *NI* (nonidentifying). Discuss why the clauses are identifying or nonidentifying with a partner.

1 *Liberty Leading the People,* <u>which hangs in the Louvre,</u> was painted by Eugene Delacroix. ____NI____

2 The painting includes Marianne, who represents the victory of the French Republic over the monarchy. _____

3 Marianne, whose image appears on small stamps and euro coins, is also depicted as a statue at Place de la République in Paris. _____

4 Botticelli's *Venus with Three Graces,* which is also located in the Louvre, is a fresco. _____

5 Fresco is a method of mural painting that is done with water-based paints on wet plaster. _____

6 The painting that Botticelli painted on the walls of the Tuscan Villa Lemmi is located in the same room as Luini's *Adoration of the Magi*. _____

7 People who visit the Louvre can use cameras and video recorders, but not flash photography. _____

8 The Louvre is the museum where parts of the movie *The Da Vinci Code* were filmed. _____

LISTENING 2

PREPARING TO LISTEN

UNDERSTANDING KEY VOCABULARY

PRISM Digital Workbook

1 Read the definitions. Complete the sentences with the correct form of the words in bold.

> **analyze** (v) to study something in a systematic and careful way
> **appreciate** (v) to recognize how good or useful something is
> **display** (v) to show something in a public place
> **focus on** (phr v) to give a lot of attention to one particular person, subject, or thing
> **interpret** (v) to describe the meaning of something, often after having examined it in order to do so
> **reject** (v) to refuse to accept or believe something
> **restore** (v) to return something to an earlier condition
> **reveal** (v) to show something that was previously hidden or secret

1 I don't think you fully _____ the talent of the artist.

2 We should scientifically _____ the painting to determine its age.

3 I hope the artist's speech will _____ the inspiration for his work.

4 I would proudly _____ the artwork in my gallery.

5 It would be difficult to correctly _____ the symbolism in the painting.

6 I firmly _____ the idea that the graffiti artist is a criminal.

7 Some artists work to _____ old or destroyed art to its former glory.

8 The artist's name is a secret; the gallery owner will _____ the identity at the grand opening.

2 You are going to listen to an informal debate about public art. Before you listen, discuss the questions with a partner.

1 A local city government is considering using the budget to build a recreation center rather than paying for new public art. Which do you think is more important for a community? Why?
2 What arguments can you think of for paying for public art?
3 What arguments can you think of for building a recreation center instead?

WHILE LISTENING

3 ▶ 7.3 Listen to the informal debate. Take notes on the participants and their opinions.

person	opinions
Robert	
Lisa	
Ahmad	
Marco	
Pei	
Claudia	

4 Check (✔) the opinions mentioned in the discussion. Use your notes from Exercise 3 to help you.

1 Maintaining the sculpture costs too much money. ☐
2 Public buildings could be sold instead of the sculpture. ☐
3 Art is an important part of any culture. ☐
4 Removing public art could cause big problems in the city. ☐
5 The sculpture is a safety concern. ☐
6 Public art could become a tourist attraction. ☐
7 A private donation has been made that will pay for a recreation center. ☐
8 A balance needs to exist between leisure activities and public art. ☐

5 ▶ **7.3** Listen to the debate again and complete the notes. Then compare notes in pairs.

Statement 1: Public art is a waste of money.
Response 1.1: Art can have a very positive effect on people.
Response 1.2: Art is an important part of any culture.
Response 1.3: We don't know if we can sell the sculpture.
Decision 1: We need to find out (1)_____ and get an art expert to (2)_____ .

Statement 2: If we don't commission public art, we need to put something in its place.
Response 2.1: Build the recreation center instead.
Response 2.2: We'd need to (3)_____ .
Decision 2: Let's put together (4)_____ .

Statement 3: The public art causes a public safety issue. Kids (5)_____ .
Response 3.1: I wonder if it's (6)_____ that's the problem.
Response 3.2: Moving it might solve the problem. It is just costing us money for repairs.
Decision 3: We should consider moving the sculpture to (7)_____ .

Statement 4: What if the city does not commission more art or build the recreation center?
Response 4.1: The money would be put back into the budget, and we'd have to (8)_____ .
Response 4.2: Our children need to (9)_____ . We need to balance art and leisure in the lives of our children.
Decision 4: We need to (10)_____ in more detail.

Intersection II by Richard Serra

POST-LISTENING

SKILLS

Distinguishing fact from opinion

A fact is a piece of information that is known to be true. An opinion is an individual's ideas or beliefs about a subject. Ideally, in a debate everyone agrees on the facts so that the debate can focus on opinions.

Graffiti began in Philadelphia. (fact)

Graffiti ruins the city landscape. (opinion)

6 Are these sentences facts or opinions? Write *F* (fact) or *O* (opinion).

1 The total bill for cleaning and repairs has come to more than $7,000. _____
2 Constantly cleaning and restoring a piece of art is not an appropriate way to spend public money. _____
3 We had 400,000 visitors to our art museum last year. _____
4 We don't know exactly how much the art is worth. _____
5 We can replace the art with something that will be popular. _____
6 I don't think we'll be able to find anything that everyone likes. _____
7 Kids have been damaging the sculpture almost every night. _____
8 The shopping center will be a great place to display public art. _____

7 Work with a partner. Write one opinion about each fact.

1 There is graffiti on the sculpture.

_____

2 Kids climb on the existing sculpture.

_____

3 The town is building a recreation center.

_____

4 Repairing and restoring the sculpture costs thousands of dollars.

_____

DISCUSSION

SYNTHESIZING

8 Work with a partner. Discuss the questions.

1 Which places near you display public art? What is your opinion of the artwork? Do you think most people have the same opinion?
2 Why do you think these places have put art on display?
3 Who pays for the art and its preservation? Do you agree that this is a good use of public money? Why or why not?
4 Use your notes from Listening 1 and Listening 2 to answer the following question. Some cities pay artists to paint graffiti on their buildings. What makes this different from the graffiti mentioned in Listening 1?

SPEAKING

CRITICAL THINKING

At the end of this unit, you are going to do the Speaking Task below.

> Have an informal debate about whether or not public money should be spent on public art.

SKILLS
Debate statements and responses

In a debate, a *statement* is an expression of a position, opinion, or suggestion on the topic. A *response* is a reaction to the statement that has been made. Participants in a debate respond to an initial statement and any further responses before a decision can be reached.

1 Look back at Exercise 5 from Listening 2. Notice how the debate is structured. Then match the parts of a debate to the sentences from the debate.

ANALYZE ◮

1 Statement
2 Response 1
3 Response 2
4 Decision

a Tax dollars should be used to buy public art.
b I don't think tax dollars should buy art because not everyone likes it.
c Let's put together a proposal.
d You could say that, but I think we could probably find some piece of art that would be popular.

SKILLS
Taking notes for a debate

In a debate, you need to be prepared to give reasons and evidence for your position. You will also need to think about how you can prove that the opposing side's reasons are weak or illogical. When you prepare for a debate, be sure to do some research beforehand and take notes on the following:

> 1. Your statement
>   a. Find reasons to support your statement.
>   b. Find facts or examples to support your reasons.
> 2. The opposing statement
>   a. Think of reasons that the opposing side may use to support their statement.
>   b. Find weaknesses in the opposing side's reasons – facts or examples that weaken or disprove them.

Coming to a debate with thorough notes will help you remember the information you need to support your statement and weaken the opposing side's position.

2 Work with a partner. Think of four more reasons to support each statement in the table. Write the reasons next to the numbers.

statement 1: Tax dollars *should* be spent on public art.	statement 2: Tax dollars *should not* be spent on public art.
1 Public art can attract tourists and boost the local economy.	1 There are more important things to spend tax dollars on, like police and emergency services.
2	2
3	3
4	4
5	5

▲ EVALUATE

3 Evaluate your reasons from Exercise 2. Decide which statement and reasons you agree with the most. Write the statement as an opinion:

Tax dollars *should / should not* be spent on public art because

_____ .

This will be the opinion you defend in the Speaking Task at the end of this unit.

▲ ANALYZE

4 With your partner, think of facts and examples to use as evidence to support the reasons you wrote for your statement. Write them in the table.

5 Look back at the reasons you wrote for the opposing statement in Exercise 2. With your partner, think of some facts or examples you could use to weaken or disprove these reasons. Write them in the table.

PREPARATION FOR SPEAKING

LANGUAGE FOR DEBATES

Expressing contrasting opinions

In a debate or discussion, people may state opinions that you disagree with. If you want to persuade people that your opinion is correct or that what the other person said is untrue, you can introduce the opposing opinion and then express your own contrasting opinion using the expressions below.

Opinion the speaker disagrees with

At first glance, it looks/seems as if ...
Many people think (that) ...
People tend to believe (that) ...
We assume (that) ...   *public art is popular.*
It looks like ...
We take it for granted that ...
Some people say ...
It seems like ...

Speaker's opinion

But in fact, ... / The fact is ...
However, ...
Actually, ...
But actually, ...   *not everyone wants to spend tax*
In reality, ...   *dollars on art.*
The truth/fact of the matter is ...
Nevertheless, ...
Even so ...

At first glance, it looks as if graffiti is on the rise in our city, **but actually**, it is on the decline.

1 Read the example sentence and answer the questions.

This looks like spray painting, **but in fact**, it's a very artistic piece of work.

1 What does the speaker think of the work?
2 Which expression in bold signals the opinion that the speaker disagrees with?
3 Which expression in bold signals the speaker's opinion?

2 Work in pairs. Take turns saying the example sentence in the explanation box, replacing the bold phrases with other phrases from the box.

PRISM **Digital** Workbook

3 Work in pairs. Take turns giving contrasting opinions. Use the words in parentheses to help you.

1 **Statement 1:** A lot of money is spent on public art.
Statement 2: Only 0.5% of public money is spent on art. (We assume that ... ; but in fact)
We assume that a lot of money is spent on public art, but in fact only 0.5% of public money is spent on art.

2 **Statement 1:** Public art has no long-term cost.
Statement 2: Cleaning and maintenance need to be considered. (Many people think that ... ; However)

3 **Statement 1:** The new sculpture is very popular.
Statement 2: A thousand people have signed a petition to have it removed. (It seems like ... ; but actually)

4 **Statement 1:** The government wasted a lot of money on the sculpture.
Statement 2: It was donated to the city. (It looks like ... ; The fact of the matter is)

SKILLS

Restating somebody's point

In an informal debate or discussion, speakers sometimes restate another person's point, either because they aren't sure they've understood it and they want to clarify it or because they want to call attention to it and argue against it.

PRISM **Digital** Workbook

4 Read the conversations. Does speaker A feel speaker B is asking for clarification or starting an argument? Write *C* (clarification) or *A* (argument).

1 **A:** I think we should start over again.
B: Start over again? Do you mean reject all three of the applications?
A: No, I think we should consider them all, but let's take a break first.
_____

2 **A:** It's clear to me that we shouldn't invest in art right now. We don't have the money.
B: We don't have the money? So what you're saying is that public art isn't important.
A: That's not exactly what I meant; art is important, but there just isn't any money in the budget right now. _____

3 **A:** That painting is nothing but graffiti.
B: Nothing but graffiti? In other words, you don't think it's art.
A: Exactly. Art is in museums, not in public spaces. _____

4 **A:** We can spend $10,000 a year on art for the next three years.
B: $10,000 a year? So, if I understand you correctly, our total artwork budget is $30,000, then?
A: Yes, that's right. _____

5 Work in pairs. Take turns reading the statements and restating them, either to clarify the statement or argue against it. Use the expressions in Exercise 4 to help you.

1 Pablo Picasso is the best artist the world has ever seen.
2 Fashion designers are artists, and clothes are works of art.
3 I don't think the government should spend any money on public art.

SKILLS

Language for hedging

Hedging makes speakers sound less direct and more polite when responding to a statement that they do not agree with. Hedging reduces the risk of someone arguing with you because you are weakening your statements. You can add modals like *may, might, can*, and *could* for hedging.

A: Public art is a waste of time and money.
B: Well, **I'm not an expert, but** I have heard that some professional psychologists say that art **might** benefit your health.

Speaker B hedges by clearly stating that he or she is not an expert before giving an opinion, and uses the modal *might* to weaken the statement.

Here are some other hedging phrases you can use to make a statement or respond.

Hedges for making a statement	Hedges for responding
Personally, I'm not really sure …	You could say that; however, …
I'm not an expert, but …	That's true in part, but I think …
All I know is …	You may be right, but I wonder if …
For me, …	I see what you're saying, but maybe …

6 Work with a partner. Look at the opinions and responses in the table. Take turns giving opinions and responding. Use hedging language to make the opinions and responses more polite.

	student A: opinions	student B: responses
1	I don't think this picture represents anything important.	I disagree. It gives us something to think about.
2	Making art isn't as important as making money.	I disagree. Making art is an important form of human expression.
3	We shouldn't install this sculpture.	I disagree. It would be very popular with the students.
4	Painting graffiti is a crime.	Not all graffiti-style painting is a crime.

PRONUNCIATION FOR SPEAKING

Stress in hedging language

When using hedging language, the speaker usually stresses two elements in a sentence. One is the expression that acknowledges the other speaker's statement. When a modal is used to acknowledge the other speaker's original opinion, it is usually stressed. The other statement is the speaker's opinion, where often the pronoun *I* or *me* is stressed.

That <u>might</u> be true in part, but <u>I</u> think ...

PRISM Digital Workbook

7 ▶ 7.4 Listen to the hedging language. Underline the stressed words or phrases. The first one is done for you.

1 Personally, <u>I'm</u> not really sure ...
2 I'm not an expert, but ...
3 All I know is ...
4 For me, ...
5 You could say that; however, actually ...
6 That's true in part, but I think ...
7 You may be right, but I wonder if ...
8 I see what you're saying, but maybe ...

8 Work with a partner. Take turns giving opinions about art and responding with the hedging language from Exercise 7. Be sure to stress the underlined words.

SPEAKING TASK

PRISM Digital Workbook

Have an informal debate about whether or not public money should be spent on public art.

PREPARE

1 Look back at the table in Critical Thinking. Add any new reasons or evidence. Highlight your three strongest reasons – you will use them during the debate.

2 Look at the reasons and evidence you wrote for the opposing side in Critical Thinking. Think of ways to show that you disagree with those ideas. Write sentences using language for expressing contrasting opinions or hedging.

3 Refer to the Task Checklist below as you prepare for your debate.

TASK CHECKLIST	✔
Express contrasting opinions.	
Use hedging language while giving opinions and when responding to other people's opinions.	
Restate other speakers' points if relevant.	

PRACTICE

4 Work with a partner who chose the same side. Practice giving your statements and reasons.

DISCUSS

5 Work with two people who chose the opposite side. Have the debate. Take notes in the table to help you address other people's points. Could you come to any decisions or identify any next steps in your debate? Why or why not?

Public money *should* be spent on public art.	Public money *should not* be spent on public art.
1	1
2	2
3	3
Group decision:	

ON CAMPUS

CHOOSING A MAJOR

PREPARING TO LISTEN

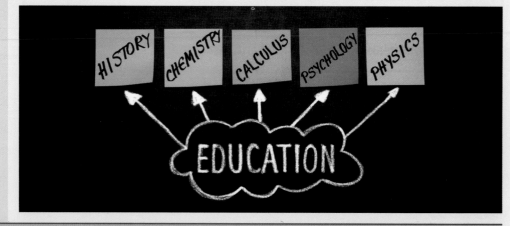

After studying in college for one or two years, most students *declare a major*. A major is a specialized field of study. Students take a number of *courses*, or classes, in one area such as biology, communications, or business.

1 Work in small groups. Discuss the questions.

   1 Imagine you are choosing a major to study in college. Which majors interest you? Why?

   2 Which of the factors below do you think are most important in choosing a major?

> family expectations   how long the course takes   your interests
> opportunities for employment   opportunities to earn money   your abilities

WHILE LISTENING

2 ▶ 7.5 Listen to the interview with a career advisor. Which factor above does she emphasize?

3 ▶ 7.5 Read the statements. Then listen to the audio again. Write *T* (true), *F* (false), or *DNS* (does not say). Correct the false sentences.

   _____ **1** Your major should be a subject that you like.

   _____ **2** You should choose your major as soon as possible after you start college.

   _____ **3** It's very important to think about how much money you will earn after you graduate.

_____ 4 It's a good idea to choose something that you are good at.

_____ 5 Your parents can often help you decide what to study.

_____ 6 A summer job can help you decide your major.

_____ 7 Everyone gets jobs in the fields that they studied in college.

_____ 8 Your choice of major is less important than the skills that you learn in college.

4 Work in small groups. Discuss the questions.

1 Do you agree with the advice in the interview?

2 Do you think that summer jobs give students a better idea of what to study? Why or why not?

3 How important is your major when choosing a career? Why?

PRACTICE

5 Read the advice for students on choosing a major. Match each piece of advice with two strategies.

1 Advice: Explore your interests and abilities.

Strategies: _____ _____

2 Advice: Research the major and the field of study.

Strategies: _____ _____

3 Advice: Use the resources that are available at your college.

Strategies: _____ _____

a Read the college catalog carefully to know which courses are required.

b Speak to an advisor in the department to discuss your schedule.

c Take a wide variety of general education classes.

d Find out about job opportunities in the field.

e Think about your hobbies and interests outside school.

f Visit the career office to find out about job opportunities.

REAL-WORLD APPLICATION

6 Choose a field of study (communications, computer science, psychology, etc.) that interests you. Research the field of study on the websites of different colleges and universities. Answer the questions.

1 What majors are offered in this field?

2 Choose one major. What courses do students usually have to take?

3 Would you like to study this major? Why or why not?

Report your findings to the class or in small groups.

LEARNING OBJECTIVES

Listening skill	Understand specific observations and generalizations
Pronunciation	Consonant reductions and joined vowels; contrastive stress in numbers and comparisons
Speaking skill	Reference data in a presentation
Speaking Task	Give a presentation using graphical data
On Campus	The world of work

ACTIVATE YOUR KNOWLEDGE

Work with a partner. Discuss the questions.

1 What do you think you will able to do when you reach old age that you cannot do now?

2 What can you do now that you will no longer be able to do when you reach old age?

3 Do you think older people should be allowed to continue working for as long as they like? Why or why not?

WATCH AND LISTEN

PREPARING TO WATCH

ACTIVATING YOUR KNOWLEDGE

1 Work with a partner. Discuss the questions.

1 In your country, what are typical activities for older people?
2 Do you think it is good for older people to have part-time jobs? Why or why not?
3 Why do you think some older people have a difficult time leaving work?

PREDICTING CONTENT USING VISUALS

2 Look at the pictures from the video. Answer the questions.

1 Which pictures best represent a typical retired person today?
2 Are most retired people in good health? Why or why not?

GLOSSARY

boomer (n) a person born during a "baby boom" in the U.S. between 1947 and 1961

adventurous (adj) willing to try new or difficult things

shuffleboard (n) a game in which people push disks along a surface with long-handled sticks to score points

amenity (n) a building, piece of equipment, or service that is provided for people's comfort or enjoyment

recession (n) a period when the economy of a country is not doing well

401(k) (n) an investment account in the U.S. that working people pay part of their income into for use when they retire; a type of private pension

WHILE WATCHING

3 ▶ Watch the video. Write *T* (true) or *F* (false) next to the statements. Then correct the false statements.

_____ 1 Gordon and Peggy live in a retirement community 45 minutes from Phoenix.

_____ 2 Houses in their neighborhood sell for about $200,000.

_____ 3 70% of boomers believe they are more active than their parents were in retirement.

_____ 4 Many boomers continue to work due to a financial loss during the recession.

4 ▶ Watch again. Match the people to their ideas about retirement.

1 Gordon Feld   **a** Doing nothing does not sound exciting.
2 Ben Tracy (reporter)   **b** Retirement should be adventurous.
3 woman (realtor)   **c** Boomers want amenities where they live.
4 Jerry Axton   **d** Their expectations include living long.

5 Complete the statements to describe the people in the video.

1 Peggy and Gordon Feld _____ .
   a like to participate in exciting activities
   b like quiet activities

2 Today's baby boomers _____ .
   a require more health care and financial advising than previous generations
   b are in better health than retired people in previous generations

3 Jerry Axton _____ .
   a enjoys working
   b would prefer not to work

DISCUSSION

6 Work with a partner. Discuss the questions.

1 Which of the activities in the video would you like to participate in when you retire?

2 How do you think your retirement will be similar to or different from those of the people in the video?

LISTENING

LISTENING 1

PREPARING TO LISTEN

1 You are going to listen to a finance podcast. Before you listen, discuss the questions in a group.

1 What is the age of retirement in your country? Do you think that is too old, too young, or just right? Why?

2 Do people in your country save money for retirement? How do they usually do it?

2 Read the definitions. Complete the sentences with correct form of the words in bold.

> **asset** (n) something valuable that is owned by a person, a business, or an organization
>
> **dependent** (n) a person who is financially supported by another person
>
> **ensure** (v) to make something certain to happen
>
> **generation** (n) all of the people of about the same age within a society or within a particular family
>
> **pension** (n) a sum of money paid regularly to a person who has retired
>
> **permit** (v) to allow something; to make something possible
>
> **property** (n) land and buildings owned by someone
>
> **retirement** (n) the point at which someone stops working, especially because of having reached a particular age

1 Many Americans look forward to _____ , when they stop working permanently and have more leisure time.

2 There were three _____ of my family at the party: my grandparents, my parents, and me.

3 The management company for the seniors' housing complex does not _____ people under the age of 55 to live there.

4 My brother has two _____ – his young son and his baby daughter.

5 One part of a nurse's job at an assisted living home is to _____ that the residents get the medications they need.

6 My father will start receiving his _____ when he turns 68 years old. The money will help him live comfortably without having to work.

7 Many people decide to buy a home rather than rent because they want to own _____ .

8 My grandparents have a large amount of _____ in Nova Scotia. Their farm takes up four acres of land.

WHILE LISTENING

3 ▶ 8.1 Listen to the podcast about retirement and the elderly. Check (✔) the topics discussed. Then compare with a partner.

LISTENING FOR MAIN IDEAS

1 a comparison of past and present retirement ☐
2 the financial and social problems of elder care ☐
3 an example of an enjoyable retirement ☐
4 problems experienced traveling abroad ☐
5 the effects of increased health and fitness ☐
6 the role of retirees in their grandchildren's lives ☐
7 a prediction about retirement ☐
8 advice on how to save money ☐

4 ▶ 8.1 Listen to the podcast again. Complete the notes with the numbers you hear.

TAKING NOTES ON DETAILS

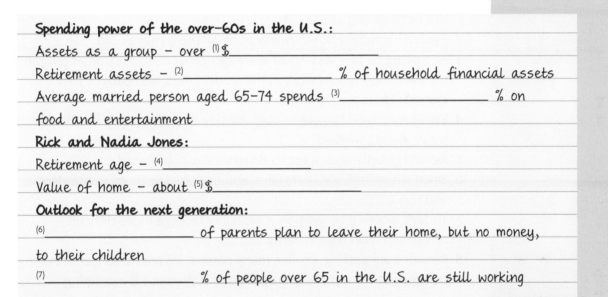

Spending power of the over-60s in the U.S.:
Assets as a group – over (1) $_____
Retirement assets – (2) _____ % of household financial assets
Average married person aged 65–74 spends (3) _____ % on food and entertainment
Rick and Nadia Jones:
Retirement age – (4) _____
Value of home – about (5) $_____
Outlook for the next generation:
(6) _____ of parents plan to leave their home, but no money, to their children
(7) _____ % of people over 65 in the U.S. are still working

POST-LISTENING

SKILLS

Understanding specific observations and generalizations

Specific observations are statements about particular people, things, or facts. *Generalizations* are broad statements about the way things usually are. Remember that a generalization is not necessarily always true. Listening for whether something is a specific observation or a generalization can tell you if it is true just in the case the speaker is referring to, or in a large number of cases.

Senior citizens are enjoying their retirement years. (generalization)
Senior citizens interviewed at the Golden River Retirement Home said they are enjoying their retirement years. (specific observation)

PRISM **Digital**
Workbook

5 Read the sentences and write *S* (specific observation) or *G* (generalization).

1 We both retired at 65. __S__

2 People nowadays don't usually think of the sixties as old. __G__

3 According to one survey, 20 years ago, most of today's older people believed they would work in the garden, read, and babysit their grandchildren. _____

4 We've managed to save enough money to permit us to live the life we've always wanted. _____

5 Retired people now want to do more exciting things! _____

6 Since we retired, we've traveled and have had years of excitement and fun. _____

7 Today's working generation is probably facing a more difficult retirement than their parents. _____

8 Pensions are getting smaller, many companies are no longer providing pensions at all, and the average age of retirement is increasing. _____

PRONUNCIATION FOR LISTENING

SKILLS

Consonant reductions and joined vowels

When speaking naturally, native speakers do not always pronounce each sound. They connect words, which may cause *consonant reductions* in which consonant sounds such as /t/ or /d/ are dropped.

twenty → "tweny"   and then → "anthen"

Native speakers may also join vowels, especially when one word ends with a vowel sound and the next word begins with a vowel sound (such as /w/ or /y/).

go out → go /w/ out   she arrived → she /y/ arrived

6 ▶ 8.2 Listen and check (✔) the correct category for the words in bold.

	vowels joined with /y/	vowels joined with /w/	dropped /d/	dropped /t/
1 ... **and because** they worked hard and saved hard for their retirement, they have plenty of money to spend.				
2 According **to one** survey, 20 years ago, most of today's older people believed they would work in the garden, read, and babysit their grandchildren.				
3 They **understand that** the money is ours to spend.				
4 They **also understand** that as long as we're in shape and healthy, we might as well enjoy life.				
5 **We are** not planning on selling it, so they'll get that eventually.				
6 I think our parents' generation thought it was really important to save for the **next generation**.				
7 People who have exercised **and eaten** a good diet throughout their lives have plenty of energy to enjoy life, no matter what age they retire at.				

7 Work in pairs. Practice saying the sentences in Exercise 6 using consonant reductions and joined vowels.

DISCUSSION

8 Work with a partner. Discuss the questions.

1 Do you think parents should stop providing for their children at some point in their lives? Why or why not?
2 What do you hope to give your own children in the future?
3 What can children do for their parents when they become adults?

VERBS WITH INFINITIVES OR GERUNDS

Some verbs can be followed by infinitives (*to* + base form of a verb), some verbs can be followed by gerunds (verb + *-ing*), and some verbs can be followed by either.

Common examples of verbs followed by infinitives are *agree, arrange, consent, manage, offer, refuse, threaten*, and *want*.

We live close to both our daughters and **offer to babysit** our grandchildren regularly.

After some verbs in active sentences, an object goes before the infinitive. The object performs the action on the infinitive. Common examples of these verbs are *advise, allow, convince, encourage, get, persuade, prepare, teach, tell, urge*, and *warn*.

Our savings **allow us to live** the life we've always wanted.

Other verbs that follow this pattern are *cause, enable, entitle, live, persuade*, and *save*.

Common examples of verbs followed by gerunds are *avoid, consider, enjoy, finish, practice, recommend*, and *suggest*.

We **will consider traveling** after retirement since we will have more time.

Some verbs can be followed by either an infinitive or a gerund. Examples of these include *begin, continue, like, prefer, hate, love*, and *start*.
Alan **began to think** about when he would retire.
Alan **began thinking** about when he would retire.

PRISM **Digital** Workbook

1 Correct the sentences.

1 We always advise our daughters enjoy life.

_____

2 We want encourage to other people to retire early.

_____

3 We managed for save enough money when we were working.

_____

4 We would not to consent go into a retirement home.

_____

5 We refuse for spend our retirement at home.

_____

6 I won't force to my children take care of me.

_____

7 We do not need to avoid to retire because we saved a lot of money when we were working.

_____

8 The financial coach wants that you work until you are 65 years old.

_____

2 Circle the correct verb forms to complete the sentences.

1 Juliana agreed *to visit / visiting* her grandchildren once a week after she retired.

2 Mikhail and Margarita recommend *to go / going* to Cancún to celebrate our retirement.

3 We arranged *to meet / meeting* a financial coach to make sure we had enough money saved before retirement.

4 We were persuaded *to babysit / babysitting* our grandchildren after we stopped working every day.

5 When José finishes *to work / working*, he is moving to Florida because the weather is warmer.

6 My grandmother enjoys *to garden / gardening* and spends more time in the backyard than she did before she stopped working.

7 Tomás manages *to save / saving* an extra 50 dollars a month; he wants to use the money to buy a house when he retires.

8 Annalise practices *to play / playing* the piano more now that she is retired.

3 Rewrite the sentences using the verbs in parentheses. In some items, more than one answer is possible.

1 My children said they would let me live with them when I'm old. (offer)
   My children offered to let me live with them when I'm old.

2 Trina wanted to move to a new city. (consider)

_____

3 Her pension was generous, so she could retire comfortably. (allow)

_____

4 We would never leave our children without any inheritance. (threaten)

_____

PREPARING TO LISTEN

1 You are going to listen to two students give presentations about the elderly in their countries. Before you listen, read the sentences and circle the correct definition for the words in bold.

1 Some children assume **responsibility** for their elderly parents.
   a the urge to reject someone
   b the duty to take care of someone or something
   c the role of a young child

2 I want to visit Turkey because that is where my **ancestors** are from.
   a people related to you who lived a long time ago
   b your grandchildren
   c people who are not related to you, but who have a common interest

3 Juan's father is a good **provider**; he works hard to make sure his family has everything they need.
   a someone who takes money for personal use
   b someone who brings money and resources to a family
   c someone who teaches academic subjects

4 My brothers **contribute** half of their paychecks to the household bills.
   a earn
   b take money away from someone
   c help by providing money or support

5 Residents of the retirement home can **participate** in a variety of activities and social events.
   a avoid taking part in something
   b think about doing something
   c become involved in an activity

6 Many adults **devote** their free time to helping their elderly parents.
   a avoid doing something
   b use time, energy, etc., for a particular purpose
   c forget to do something important

7 The **institution** where my grandfather lives has excellent nursing care.
   a place where an organization takes care of people for a period of time
   b apartment complex
   c government building

8 Surveys **indicate** that more and more elderly people are moving into retirement homes.
   a make a false claim
   b keep information a secret from the public
   c show, point, or make clear in another way

2 Work with a partner. Discuss the questions.

1 What challenges do the elderly face in modern society?
2 What are the advantages of institutions for the elderly? The disadvantages?
3 What are the advantages of caring for elderly relatives at home? The disadvantages?

3 Compare your answers with another pair.

USING YOUR KNOWLEDGE

WHILE LISTENING

4 ▶ 8.3 Listen to two students, Mika and Ahmet, give presentations on the situation for elderly people in their countries. Create a T-chart to take notes on the information each student presents.

5 Use your notes from Exercise 4 to answer the questions. Then compare answers with a partner.

1 Where is each speaker from?
Mika: _____
Ahmet: _____
2 Who focuses on the changing situation of the elderly? _____
3 Who focuses on how the elderly are cared for? _____
4 What are their main points?
Mika: _____
_____
Ahmet: _____
_____

TAKING NOTES ON MAIN IDEAS

6 ▶ 8.3 Use your notes from Exercise 4 to complete the details in the table. Then listen again to check your answers.

	Mika	Ahmet
country		
population today		
% over 65 today		
% of households with older people	no information	
expected population in 2050		no information
expected % age over 65 in 2050		no information

POST-LISTENING

7 Work in pairs. Are the situations following the words and phrases in bold causes or effects? Write C (cause) or E (effect).

1 This increase will **result in** more elderly people that need care. _____
2 My grandparents live with us **because** they need more help than when they were younger. _____
3 When older relatives move in, it **leads to** a child's role changing from dependent to caregiver. _____
4 The population increase **stems from** the fact that people are living longer. _____
5 Living closely together can **raise** tensions. _____
6 Moving elderly people into nursing homes **allows** the younger generation to continue their lives unchanged. _____

DISCUSSION

8 Work with a partner. Discuss the questions.

1 How are the elderly cared for in your country?
2 Has this changed in the past 20 years? If so, how?
3 Do you think it will change in the next 20 years? Why or why not?
4 Use your notes from Listening 1 and Listening 2 to answer the following questions. What will you do after you retire? Who do you think you will live with? What will your lifestyle be like?

SPEAKING

CRITICAL THINKING

At the end of this unit, you are going to do the Speaking Task below.

▌ Give a presentation on how aging has changed a country's population over time and the impact this is likely to have on its society in the future.

ANALYZE ▲

SKILLS

Line graphs

Line graphs are used to show changes in data over time. It is important to look at any significant or unusual features in a line graph as well as the main data trends.

1 Look at the line graph. Answer the questions.

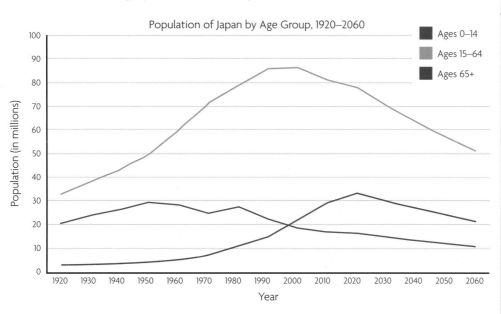

Population of Japan by Age Group, 1920–2060

- Ages 0–14
- Ages 15–64
- Ages 65+

1 What was Japan's population age 65 and older in the year 2010?

_____

2 What was Japan's population age 14 and under in 2010?

_____

3 What will Japan's population age 65 and older be in 2050?

_____

4 Which population group will be the largest in 2050?

_____

5 As of 2010, which population group is the lowest and will continue to decrease over time?

_____

2 Look at the graph in Exercise 1 again. What might happen to the populations after 2060? Make three predictions.

Prediction 1: _____

_____

Prediction 2: _____

_____

Prediction 3: _____

_____

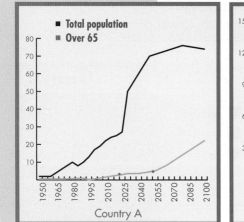 EVALUATE

3 Split into three groups. Each group will look at one country: A, B, or C. In your group, look at the graph for your country. Answer the questions and take notes.

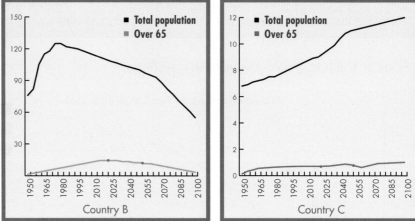

1 What are the main points or trends that your graph shows?

_____

_____

_____

_____

_____

2 Is there a relationship between any of the data in your graph (e.g., cause and effect)?

_____

_____

_____

_____

_____

4 Look at the additional information about your country below. Answer the questions in your group and take notes.

1 How does this information correspond with the data on the graph?

_____

_____

2 Is it supported by the main points that you found?

_____

_____

3 Is it supported by any significant or unusual features in the graph?

_____

_____

Country A

- In country A, many young people have recently begun moving to the city, so rural populations are becoming more elderly.
- At 2%, the percentage of the population age 65+ is relatively small and almost all elderly people are cared for by their families.
- The government has no plans to provide institutions for elderly people.

Country B

- For people in country B, it is normal for adult children to leave home and live away from their parents.
- Most elderly people are cared for by institutions. This enables younger generations to continue working, knowing they are well-cared for.
- The government provides institutions for elderly people in order to help families who cannot afford to pay for their care.

Country C

- For people in country C, adult children usually settle near their parents so they can take care of them in old age.
- About 30% of elderly people are cared for by institutions.
- Because of a predicted increase in the population age 65+ in the next 50 years, the government has started a program to build institutions for elderly people.

5 With your group, make predictions about what might happen to the country's population after 2100.

_____

_____

_____

REFERENCING DATA IN A PRESENTATION

SKILLS

Explaining details and trends in a graph

You can use specific language to explain the types of details and trends shown in a graph. Using these phrases will help the listener understand the data better.

increases	decreases	continuous changes
skyrocket / spike	decrease / fall	fluctuate
peak at	drop	stabilize
a steady increase	a steady decrease	remain steady

PRISM Digital Workbook

1 Look at the line graphs. Match the descriptions to the correct country (A or B).

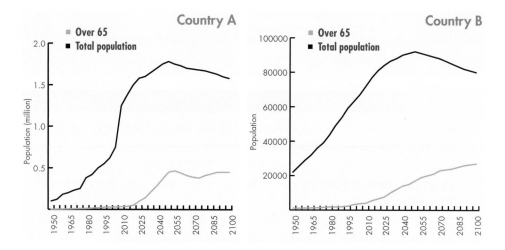

1 As you can see in the graph, between 2010 and 2080, the population of over-65s **will skyrocket** from 4,000 to 24,000 people. _____

2 If you look at the graph, we can see the population **peaks at** 1.78 million people in 2050. _____

3 Between 2055 and 2070, the population of over-65s **is probably going to drop** from 466,000 to 390,000. _____

4 If you look at the data provided, you can see that the growth in population **remains steady** from 1950 to 2050. _____

5 After peaking in 2055, the population of over-65s **will fluctuate and then stabilize** at about 450,000 people. _____

6 After **a steady increase** in population between 2010 and 2050, the population **is predicted to fall** slowly. _____

2 Work with a partner. Look at the phrases in bold in Exercise 1. These are different ways to describe details and trends in a graph. Use these phrases to describe other details and trends you may notice in the graphs.

After an increase in the population of over-65s, ...

Explaining causes and effects

Explaining causes and effects to your audience helps them understand why information is important and how different pieces of information are connected.

PRISM Digital Workbook

3 Match the sentence halves.

1 The steady increase in population between 1950 and 2000 was the result of ... _____
2 The sharp rise in population between 2005 and 2010 was brought about by ... _____
3 The predicted decrease in population from 2050 onward can be traced back to ... _____
4 The number of over-65s will increase steeply after 2020 because of ... _____
5 Immigration and improvements in health care between 1950 and the present account for ... _____

a families deciding to have fewer children today.
b huge improvements in health care today.
c a high level of immigration during that period.
d a steady population increase from 22 million to nearly 80 million.
e a large number of young people deciding to have children.

4 For each expression, use phrases from the table to write cause and effect sentences. More than one answer may be possible.

effect		cause
People living longer	1 was the result of	improvements in medical care.
A population decrease	2 was brought about by	an increase in people over 65.
A population increase	3 can be traced back to	people moving out of the country.
The steady population	4 was due to	the high number of people over 65.

People living longer was the result of improvements in medical care.

1 _____

2 _____

3 _____

4 _____

PRONUNCIATION FOR SPEAKING

SKILLS

Contrastive stress in numbers and comparisons

A speaker comparing numbers usually stresses the numbers and the comparison words to emphasize the importance of the numbers.

By 2100, the youth population will make up 12 percent of the country's total population. This figure is significantly higher than the figure of 3 percent predicted for 2050.

PRISM Digital Workbook

5 ▶ 8.4 Listen to the sentence pairs. Underline the stressed words and numbers. The first one is done for you.

1 Today, the over-65s make up 2.5% of Country A's total population. This figure is smaller than the figure of 7% for Country B.

2 The population of Country B will be 77 million in 2050. This number is much larger than the figure of 1.4 million for Country A in 2050.

3 By 2050, Country A's population will rise to 1.78 million people. The population for Country B also peaks in 2050 with 9.2 million people.

6 Work with a partner. Practice saying the sentences in Exercise 5 with the underlined words and numbers stressed.

SPEAKING TASK

▶ Give a presentation on how aging has changed a country's population over time and the impact this is likely to have on its society in the future.

PREPARE

1 Look back at your notes about the country you chose (A, B, or C) in Critical Thinking. Add any new information.

2 Write notes on the following areas for your talk. Use language from Preparation for Speaking to help you.

   1 Presenting your data
   2 Talking about the causes and effects of your data
   3 Making predictions for the future of the country you chose

3 Refer to the Task Checklist below as you prepare your presentation.

TASK CHECKLIST	✔
Reference data in your presentation.	
Make predictions based on data.	
Explain causes and effects.	
Use contrastive stress when making comparisons.	

PRACTICE

4 Practice your presentation in your group.

PRESENT

5 Form a new group with people who have looked at the other two countries. Give your presentation to your new group. Were your presentations similar? Why or why not?

ON CAMPUS

THE WORLD OF WORK

PREPARING TO LISTEN

1 Read the definitions. Complete the text with the correct form of the words in bold.

> **graduate school** (n) a school or department where students study for a postgraduate degree
>
> **internship** (n) a period of time spent working at a job in order to get training or experience
>
> **job fair** (n) an event where people looking for a job can meet future employers
>
> **network** (v) to meet and talk to people in order to get useful information or job contacts
>
> **résumé** (n) a written statement of your educational and work experience

What are you planning to do when you graduate? Maybe you would like to go to ⁽¹⁾_____ to get a master's or doctoral degree. If you are looking for your first job, make sure that you attend the ⁽²⁾_____ on campus next week. Here you will have the opportunity to meet and ⁽³⁾_____ with potential employers. Prepare at least 20 copies of your ⁽⁴⁾_____ to give them. Some companies may not offer you a job, but they may have ⁽⁵⁾_____ positions. These are often low paid, but they are a great way to get work experience.

WHILE LISTENING

2 ▶ 8.5 Listen to the presentation at a college career center. Circle the resources on the website that the speaker mentions.

CAREER CENTER RESOURCES

| Home | Job listings | Careers | Graduates |

Upcoming Job Fairs

Volunteer Opportunities

Work and Study Abroad

Graduate Schools

Workshops:

> Strategies for a Successful Interview

> Résumé Writing for College Students

> Your Online Identity: Social Media and the Job Search

> Lecture: Working in the Software Industry

3 8.5 Listen again. Answer the questions.

  1 What kinds of jobs can students find at the career center?

  2 Why would a student take an unpaid internship?

  3 What kind of experience can students put in a résumé?

  4 Why is your online identity important?

  5 What can students do at a job fair?

  6 What resources are there for students who want to continue in college?

4 Compare your answers with a partner. Discuss the questions.

  1 Why should students visit the career center "early and often"?

  2 Which of the resources would you use?

PRACTICE

5 For each problem below, choose two resources from the career center in Exercise 2 that a student could use.

  1 "I need to find a summer job, but I've never interviewed before."

  2 "I'd like to find out about working overseas, maybe in a developing country."

  3 "I'd like to go to law school ... but I'm not sure that I want to be a lawyer."

  4 "I'd like to start my own software company!"

  5 "I'm graduating this year and I want to find a good job!"

6 Work with a partner. Imagine that you work at the career center in Exercise 2. Role-play short conversations between you and a student looking for advice.

> **A** I need to find a summer job, but I've never interviewed before.

> **B** Maybe you could look at the job listings. We also have a workshop on interview techniques.

REAL-WORLD APPLICATION

7 Choose one of the categories below, or think of your own. Visit the career center at your school or university, or look at a career center website. Find out what resources are available in that category.

Category 1: Help with interviewing, résumé writing, and online identity
Category 2: Information about jobs available on and off campus
Category 3: Help with the job search: job fairs, networking events, etc.
Category 4: Volunteer opportunities and internships
Category 5: (Your choice)

8 Work in small groups. Report your findings to the class.

GLOSSARY OF KEY VOCABULARY

Words that are part of the Academic Word List are noted with an **A** in this glossary.

UNIT 1 GLOBALIZATION

LISTENING 1

consumer A (n) a person who buys things for personal use

greenhouse (n) a building used to grow plants that need constant warmth and protection

import (v) to bring in from another country to sell or use

investigate A (v) to carefully examine something, especially to discover the truth about it

overseas A (adv) in, from, or to countries that are across the sea

produce (v) to create something or bring it into existence

purchase A (v) to buy

LISTENING 2

agriculture (n) the practice or work of farming

domestic A (adj) related to a person's own country

export A (n) a product that a country sells to another country

household (n) a group of people, often a family, who live together

process A (v) to add chemicals to a substance, especially food, in order to change it or make it last longer

source A (n) the place where a product is made or created

transportation A (n) the movement of people or goods from one place to another

UNIT 2 EDUCATION

LISTENING 1

academic A (adj) related to subjects that require thinking and studying

acquire A (v) to get or receive something

advisor (n) someone whose job is to give advice about a subject

internship (n) a short time spent training at a job in order to become qualified to do it

mechanical (adj) related to machines

specialist (n) someone with a lot of skill or experience in a subject

understanding (n) knowledge about a subject

vocational (adj) related to a particular type of work

LISTENING 2

complex A (adj) involving a lot of different but related parts

manual A (adj) involving the use of the hands

medical A (adj) concerned with the treatment of disease and injury

physical A (adj) related to someone's body rather than the mind

practical (adj) relating to experience, real situations, or actions rather than ideas or imagination

professional A (adj) connected with a job that needs special education or training

secure A (adj) dependable; not likely to change

technical A (adj) relating to the knowledge, machines, or methods used in science and industry

UNIT 3 MEDICINE

LISTENING 1

contract (A) (v) to catch or become ill with a disease

factor (A) (n) a fact or situation that influences the result of something

infected (adj) having a disease as a result of the introduction of organisms such as bacteria and viruses to the body

occur (A) (v) to happen

outbreak (n) a sudden appearance of something, especially of a disease or something else dangerous or unpleasant

prevention (n) the act of stopping something from happening

recover (A) (v) to become completely well again after an illness or injury

treatment (n) something that you do to try to cure an illness or injury, especially something suggested by a doctor

LISTENING 2

clinical (adj) related to medical treatment and tests

controlled (adj) limited

data (A) (n) information or facts about something

precaution (n) an action that is taken to stop something negative from happening

prove (v) to show to be true

researcher (A) (n) a person who studies a subject in detail to discover new information about it

scientific (adj) related to science

trial (n) a test to find out how effective or safe something is

UNIT 4 THE ENVIRONMENT

LISTENING 1

adapt (A) (v) to adjust to different conditions

coastal (adj) on or related to land by the sea or ocean

conservation (n) the protection of plants, animals, and natural areas

exploit (A) (v) to use something unfairly for your own advantage

habitat (n) the natural surroundings where a plant or animal lives

impact (A) (n) the strong effect that something has on something else

modify (A) (v) to change something to make it more acceptable or less extreme

waste (n) unwanted matter or material

LISTENING 2

copper (n) a reddish-brown metal, used in electrical equipment and for making wires and coins

diamond (n) a very hard, valuable stone, often used in jewelry

harsh (adj) severe and unpleasant

minerals (n) natural substances found in the earth such as coal or gold

mining (n) the industry or activity of removing valuable substances from the earth

natural gas (n) fuel for heating or cooking that is found underground

wilderness (n) a place that is in a completely natural state without houses, industry, roads, etc.

UNIT 5 ARCHITECTURE

LISTENING 1

anticipate Ⓐ (v) to expect that something will happen

collapse Ⓐ (v) to fall down suddenly

contemporary Ⓐ (adj) happening now; modern

feature Ⓐ (n) a noticeable or important characteristic or part

investment Ⓐ (n) money that is put into something in order to make a profit

obtain Ⓐ (v) to get something, especially by a planned effort

potential Ⓐ (n) someone's or something's ability to develop, achieve, or succeed

transform Ⓐ (v) to change the appearance of something

LISTENING 2

adequate Ⓐ (adj) enough or satisfactory for a specific purpose

ambitious (adj) not easily done or achieved

appropriate Ⓐ (adj) suitable or right for a specific situation or occasion

concerned (adj) worried or anxious

controversial Ⓐ (adj) causing a lot of disagreement or argument

existing (adj) that exists or is being used at the present time

sympathetic (adj) showing support and agreement

UNIT 6 ENERGY

LISTENING 1

capacity Ⓐ (n) the amount that something can produce

consistent Ⓐ (adj) always acting in a similar way

cycle Ⓐ (n) a set of events that repeat themselves regularly in the same order

element Ⓐ (n) one part of something

generate Ⓐ (v) to produce

mainland (n) the biggest or primary part of a country, not including the islands around it

network Ⓐ (n) a group formed by connected parts

reservoir (n) a lake that stores and supplies water

LISTENING 2

consumption Ⓐ (n) the act of using, eating, or drinking something

drawback (n) a disadvantage or negative part of a situation

efficient (adj) producing good results without waste

experimental (adj) new and not tested

function Ⓐ (n) a role or purpose

limitation (n) a situation that restricts something

maintenance Ⓐ (n) the work needed to keep something in good condition

volume Ⓐ (n) the number or amount of something

UNIT 7 ART AND DESIGN

LISTENING 1

comment (A) (v) to express an opinion

composition (n) the way that people or things are arranged in a painting or photograph

creativity (A) (n) the ability to produce original and unusual ideas, or to make something new or imaginative

criticism (n) the act of giving your opinion or judgment about the good or bad qualities of something or someone, especially books, films, etc.

identity (A) (n) who someone is; the qualities that make a person different from others

remove (A) (v) to take something away from an object, group, or place

right (n) a person's opportunity to act and be treated in particular ways that the law promises to protect for the benefit of society

self-expression (n) how someone expresses their personality, emotions, or ideas, especially through art, music, or acting

LISTENING 2

analyze (A) (v) to study something in a systematic and careful way

appreciate (A) (v) to recognize how good or useful something is

display (A) (v) to show something in a public place

focus on (A) (phr v) to give a lot of attention to one particular person, subject, or thing

interpret (A) (v) to describe the meaning of something, often after having examined it in order to do so

reject (A) (v) to refuse to accept or believe something

restore (A) (v) to return something to an earlier condition

reveal (A) (v) to show something that was previously hidden or secret

UNIT 8 AGING

LISTENING 1

asset (n) something valuable that is owned by a person, a business, or an organization

dependent (n) a person who is financially supported by another person

ensure (A) (v) to make something certain to happen

generation (A) (n) all of the people of about the same age within a society or within a particular family

pension (n) a sum of money paid regularly to a person who has retired

permit (v) to allow something; to make something possible

property (n) land and buildings owned by someone

retirement (n) the point at which someone stops working, especially because of having reached a particular age

LISTENING 2

ancestor (n) a person related to you who lived a long time ago

contribute (A) (v) to help by providing money or support

devote (A) (v) to use time, energy, etc. for a particular purpose

indicate (A) (v) to show, point, or make clear in another way

institution (A) (n) a place where an organization takes care of people for a period of time

participate (A) (v) to become involved in an activity

provider (n) someone who brings money and resources to a family

responsibility (n) the duty to take care of someone or something

UNIT 1

▶ **NBA Fans in China**

Seth Doane (reporter): Good morning to you, Norah. That's right. By the end of this season, the NBA will have put together almost 150 of these international games since 1978. They're a way of building the brand overseas. To call this crowd enthusiastic would be an understatement. Security struggled to keep back fans as the Lakers entered. It felt more like Southern California than Shanghai in this stadium, where the language of sport proved universal.

Fan: Kobe ... Kobe Bryant! I love Kobe so much!

Seth Doane: An injured Kobe Bryant did not play much at Thursday's fan appreciation night, though that did not seem to matter. Kobe is huge here. The NBA says viewership in China grew 30% last year. NBA Commissioner David Stern pointed out that these 13,000 people came to watch a practice.

David Stern: China is our largest market outside the United States. It has 1.3 billion people and has been playing basketball for almost as long as the United States has.

Seth Doane: Players took in some of the sights and toured the Great Wall earlier this week. It was Golden State Warriors' point guard Stephen Curry's first trip to China.

Stephen Curry: I knew that they loved the game of basketball but to see them, you know, with Warrior jerseys everywhere, it's awesome.

Seth Doane: "Awesome" could have described the night for Xiao Wei, who unfurled a banner for Curry. Rough translation, "god of cuteness."
How was it to meet him to talk with him in person?

Xiao Wei: It's beyond imagination.

Seth Doane: Making the NBA feel closer and, of course, boosting partnerships and endorsement deals is part of the mission for David Stern.

David Stern: You see opportunity everywhere, although China is going to become the largest economy in the world in the not too distant future, so that's pretty impressive of what we're going to do.

Seth Doane: So it's important for you all to be here.

David Stern: Actually, I'm surprised that Charlie Rose isn't here doing the morning news because he's a, he's a big jock.

Seth Doane: Charlie would love to be here, I think. Yes, that's right. And the NBA expects to see double-digit revenue growth every year here in China, well into the future. Last year it's estimated they hauled in around 150 million dollars in China alone. You like whose name came, comes up courtside in Shanghai, Charlie and Norah?

Norah O'Donnell: Love that. I just have one request, Seth, and that is that banner, that "god of cuteness." Can you get one of those for me so I can get it for Charlie? He's my god of cuteness.

Seth Doane: All right, I'll look in the market downstairs.

Charlie Rose: Oh, goodness. Boy, this is great. This is really great.

Norah O'Donnell: You would have loved to have been there.

Charlie Rose: I would have. Oh, yeah. I mean I did a profile of Jeremy Lin for CBS Sports, and it's just remarkable the intensity when he went back, and how much they love him, and how all that Rockets games are now seen in China.

Norah O'Donnell: Absolutely.

🔊 **1.1**

Host: Today on *The World Close Up* – "The 11,000-Mile Fruit Salad." With globalization, the world has become a smaller place. On last week's show, we talked about how people around the world are watching foreign TV shows, wearing clothes from other countries, and working at companies with several international offices. On this week's show, let's look at how globalization allows us to taste food from different cultures around the world, without leaving the country. We don't just mean specialty products, like Turkish candies and Japanese desserts. Think about the regular groceries customers are buying every day. Where do they come from? How do they get to your supermarket? And what is the true *environmental* cost of your usual grocery list? Our reporter Darren Hayes has gone to a Food King Supermarket in southern Philadelphia to **investigate** this issue and to see just what *countries* customers are putting in their shopping carts.

Reporter: Hello, listeners. I'm here at the Food King Supermarket in southern Philadelphia. There are a lot of healthy **consumers** here, and David Green is one of them. David, can we take a look in your shopping cart? What are you buying today?

David: Mostly fruit and vegetables. I have a pineapple, some bananas, some kiwis, a mango, and tomatoes. I'm making a fruit salad for lunch because I'm watching my weight. I'm trying to eat healthfully.

Reporter: I notice on the label that the bananas are from Ecuador.

David: Yeah ... so?

Reporter: Do you mind if I check the pineapple? Hmmm ... it's from Guatemala. The kiwi comes from ... California, and the mango is from Costa Rica. David, did you realize that some of this fruit is **imported** from **overseas**?

David: Well, I guess since it's winter, we can't grow these everywhere in our country. They *have* to be imported. If they weren't, then how would we get fresh fruit in the winter?

Reporter: Good point. The global food industry – and the speed of shipping fresh foods by air – allows people all over the world to eat a huge variety of fresh fruit and vegetables all year round.

David: It's just more convenient, isn't it? Most of the fruit and vegetables I like, like peppers, mangoes, and bananas, grow in hotter climates. A lot of the fruit and vegetables that grow here in the northern part of the United States only grow in the summer.

Reporter: It *is* possible to grow fruit and vegetables from hot countries here, but they have to grow in **greenhouses** or certain parts of the country, which increases production costs. If you look at these tomatoes, which were grown on a local farm, they're almost twice the cost of the tomatoes you have here from Mexico, over 2,000 miles away.

David: I'd never pay that for a few tomatoes! Local food can be so expensive. It's not worth it.

Reporter: I know, but cheap food comes at a price. Let's look at the figures. The bananas from Ecuador must have traveled more than 2,500 miles to reach Food King Supermarket, the pineapple from Guatemala must have come more than 2,000 miles, and the Costa Rican mango nearly 2,200 miles. The kiwi from California? That must have flown about 2,300 miles. So, that's about ... 11,000 miles of air travel in one bowl! That's an incredibly long food supply chain, which is the system and things involved in the moving of a product from the place it is **produced** to the person who buys it. It's also a huge carbon footprint, which means a huge amount of pollution was produced to get this food to the shelves. When food travels, a lot of carbon dioxide pollution is produced, and most people now believe that carbon dioxide in the air is causing climate change – causing the Earth to get generally warmer.

David: I've never really thought about it that much. What about this lettuce? It's local.

Reporter: Even something that looks like it's local can have a big impact on the environment. It's far cheaper for supermarkets to have several large factories than a lot of small ones all over the country, so food grown around the country is transported to large factories to be packaged and sold. This lettuce may be local, but the farm it came from could have transported it across the country and then put it into this plastic packaging. It's sometimes then transported back to the place it was grown in the first place.

David: So, before arriving at Food King Supermarket, this local lettuce might have traveled ...

Reporter: ... maybe 300 miles? You can only really be sure how far something has traveled if you **purchase** it directly from a farm or if you grow it yourself.

David: Wow. I can't believe it. Maybe I should pay the extra money for local food ...

Reporter: Thanks for your time, David. An 11,000-mile fruit salad that comes from five different countries isn't very expensive for the consumer. But the big question is, what's the true environmental cost of such a well-traveled salad? That's all for today. Thanks for listening to *The World, Close Up*.

🔊 1.2

1 ... cheap food comes at a price.
2 An 11,000-mile fruit salad ...
3 ... what's the true environmental cost of such a well-traveled salad?

🔊 1.3

1 These agricultural products are already going abroad.
2 We grow many kinds of tea on this plantation.
3 The police regularly find illegal imports.
4 The company sewed more clothes overseas last year.
5 The bananas are timed so that they ripen together.
6 Flying the crops causes air pollution.
7 The products pass through customs easily.
8 I want to know why these routes cost more.

🔊 1.4

There hasn't been much support from the government over the issue of imported agricultural crops. There are three issues with this. First, nearly a sixth of all imported fruit cannot grow in our climate. Second, the state should help our own farmers rather than foreign growers. Finally, we should not fall into the trap of not growing enough food. What would happen if it didn't rain and we were left with a food shortage?

🔊 1.5

As globalization becomes more of a reality in our everyday lives, we can see it taking root in all aspects of life. Foreign trade and imports range from the TV shows we watch and love to the food we eat and the clothes we wear every day.

As a result, it's easier than ever to find a wide variety of imported goods in our local shops and markets. But is global trade actually unhealthy for the environment? There has been a lot of discussion in the media about imported products, and especially imported foods. Many people say that imported products may in fact harm the environment because they're shipped long distances by airplane. It has been suggested that we should choose **domestic** foods over overseas **exports** because airplanes create pollution that causes environmental problems.

Let's look at food, for instance. Experts argue that foods that are the least damaging to the environment are usually the ones grown locally. Consequently, some people believe that local foods are always more environmentally friendly and, therefore, must always be the most appropriate choice, but is this really true? Let's look at some data.

This pie chart shows the carbon footprint of the U.S. food system. First, as you can see, the largest part of the carbon footprint is the section called "**Households**," meaning the energy used in homes to store and prepare food – mostly refrigeration and cooking with gas or electrical appliances. This accounts for more than a quarter of the total carbon footprint. Second, according to the chart, the next main **source** of carbon in the U.S. food system is how companies **process** their products. Examples of this would be adding chemicals to vegetables so that they can be put into cans, or turning ingredients into ready-made meals, like frozen pizza. This makes up about one-fifth of the total. After processing, **agriculture** is the next main source of carbon emissions. Parts of the United States are cool and rainy, which means that some avocados in the U.S. must grow in greenhouses. These greenhouses are heated, which therefore produces carbon dioxide. Avocados grown in Mexico require less energy to grow because the climate in Mexico is milder, and greenhouses aren't needed.

After agriculture, wholesale and retail food sales account for 14% of the food carbon footprint. This refers to the energy used to store and sell foods in warehouses and supermarkets and so on.

After that comes food service. This basically means the energy used by restaurants and cafés to supply food to customers. Next comes emissions linked to packaging such as the containers that food is put in to be sold or transported. For example, when you purchase chicken in a U.S. supermarket, it comes in a tray and is usually wrapped in plastic. Finally, the smallest portion of energy in the U.S. food system goes to **transportation**.

So, what does this tell us about food miles? In summary, the data shows that the transportation of food definitely uses energy and produces carbon emissions, but from this evidence, we can assume that it must make up the very smallest part of the carbon footprint from food.

🔊 1.6

I'd like to talk about where your money goes when you buy a cup of coffee. There has been a lot of discussion in the media recently about fair prices for the people in countries that grow crops like coffee. Many people believe that it's not right that a cup of coffee can cost $4 or more, of which the farmers only get a few pennies. However, others have pointed out that the coffee beans are only one part of the cost of supplying a cup of coffee. They say that the other ingredients, such as milk and sugar, are also a big part of the cost of a cup of coffee. However, I would like to show that in a typical coffeehouse, the ingredients are only a small part of the overall cost. Let's look at some data. If you consider the information in this chart ...

🔊 1.7

This pie chart shows where your money goes when you buy a cup of coffee. First, as you can see, the largest part of the cost is administration, at approximately 25%. That's a quarter of the cost per cup. Second is labor, which you'll notice accounts for almost 20% of the cost. Next, tax, profit, and rent each make up about 14% of the cost, or a total of 42% of the price of your cup of coffee. Finally, I'd like to draw your attention to the three parts that are related to the product you take away – milk at over 6%, the cup, sugar, and lid at almost 5%, and the coffee itself at 2%. Together, they make up just over 10% of the price you pay.

Hello everyone. You probably know that hunger is a problem in many parts of the world. But at the same time, tons of food are thrown away every year, in landfills like the one in the picture. Today I'm going to talk a little bit about food waste and what we can do about it.

First, let's see if you can answer this question: what percentage of food is thrown away in the United States every year? What do you think? Raise your hand if you think it's 10% ... 20? 30%? ... More than 30%? You're right. In fact, 40% of the food that is bought in the U.S. is wasted. This is more than 20 pounds of food per person, per month.

Why is this a problem? Well, for one thing, consumer-driven food waste in the U.S. costs approximately 165 billion dollars a year. But did you know that food waste also contributes to climate change? This is because the organic waste in our landfills emits methane, a gas that contributes to greenhouse gases. So throwing food away is expensive in terms of the waste of resources, and also it's bad for the environment.

But there's another reason: the world simply cannot afford to throw food away. As you know, hunger is a growing problem. Worldwide, more than 900 million people suffer from hunger, and the numbers are rising. The Food and Agriculture Organization estimates that by the year 2050, we will need about 170 million more acres of farmland to feed our growing population. If we could reduce consumer-driven food waste by just 30% – that's just over a quarter – we could save roughly 100 million acres of farmland.

So, cutting food waste is a very important step towards improving the global supply of food.

What can we do to fight food waste? Well, I'm going to talk about three ways that we can all work to ...

🔊 1.9

Excerpt 1

Hello everyone. You probably know that hunger is a problem in many parts of the world. But at the same time, tons of food are thrown away every year, in landfills like the one in the picture.

Excerpt 2

First, let's see if you can answer this question: what percentage of food is thrown away in the United States every year? What do you think? Raise your hand if you think it's 10% ... 20? 30%?

Excerpt 3

Why is this a problem? Well, for one thing, consumer-driven food waste in the U.S. costs approximately 165 billion dollars a year. But did you know that food waste also contributes to climate change?

Excerpt 4

As you know, hunger is a growing problem. Worldwide, more than 900 million people suffer from hunger, and the numbers are rising.

Excerpt 5

If we could reduce consumer-driven food waste by just 30% – that's just over a quarter – we could save roughly 100 million acres of farmland.

UNIT 2

▶ **A Soybean-Powered Car**

Reporter: The star at last week's Philadelphia auto show wasn't a sports car or an economy car. It was a sports economy car. Performance and practicality under a single hood: car buyers had been waiting decades for this.

Man 1: Anything going zero to 60 in four seconds – that piques my interest.

Man 2: Yeah. I didn't think you could do that with a hybrid.

Man 3: I like that it does get 51 miles to a gallon.

Reporter: And on soybean biodiesel to boot.

Man 4: This is fabulous, what they've done.

Man 3: I think they did one hell of a job.

Reporter: So, who do we have to thank? Ford? Toyota? Ferrari? Nope. Just Victor, David, Cheeseborough, Bruce, and Cozy. These high school auto shop students, along with a handful of other kids from West Philadelphia High School, built the car as an after-school project.

It took them over a year, rummaging for parts, configuring wires, learning as they went.

Simon Houger: All these rubber mounts can mount the motor to the frame.

Reporter: Impressed? Teacher Simon Houger says, wait until you hear this.

Simon Houger: We have a number of high school dropouts. We have a number that have been removed for disciplinary reasons and they end up with us.

Reporter: Cozy Harmon was in a gang at his old school, a punk, and a terrible student.

Cozy Harmon: Grades. I was just getting by the skin of my teeth, Cs and Ds. I came here and now I'm a straight-A student.

Reporter: Really?

Cozy Harmon: Yes, sir.

Check the brakes. Put the pop up.

Simon Houger: If you give kids that have been stereotyped as not being able to do anything an opportunity to do something great, they'll step up.

Cozy Harmon: Hey, ah, Clayton, brake fluid. Cool.

Reporter: Obviously, this story says a lot about the potential of our young people. Unfortunately, it also says a lot about our auto industry, now stuck playing hybrid catch-up to the bad news bears of auto shop.

Simon Houger: Yeah. It hit me that, look, we made this work. We're not geniuses, so why aren't other people doing it?

Reporter: Cozy thinks he knows. It's big oil companies.

Cozy Harmon: Right. They're making billions upon billions of dollars, right, and then when this car sells, their billions upon billions will go down to low billions upon billions.

🔊 2.1

Ada: Hello, I'm Ada. Are you my **advisor**?

Advisor: Yes, Ada. Welcome to the advising office. Good to see you.

Ada: Hi.

Advisor: Now, I saw from your file that you're looking for advice on what to major in. Do you have any ideas?

Ada: Yes, but I'm not really sure which to choose.

Advisor: Well, what are you considering?

Ada: I like math and physics, and I'm doing well in those classes.

Advisor: Looking at your file, I couldn't agree more! You should make use of your math and physics abilities. Any ideas about what you want to study?

Ada: Well, I'm considering studying engineering.

Advisor: Ah, engineering. That's a big subject area field. Well, engineering jobs are definitely popular. The world will always need engineers! What kind of engineering are you interested in? Electrical? Civil? Computer?

Ada: I'm not sure. I've always been interested in the way things work, like cars and other machines. I'd like to study something technical, that's for sure. You know, I'm actually really interested in space flight. I'd love to build rockets and spacecraft!

Advisor: Maybe you should consider **mechanical** engineering, then – as a start anyway. That's a good, basic engineering degree – it covers the basic subjects. Mechanical engineers often go on to become

specialists in lots of different areas – aerospace engineering is just one of them. It would definitely be a way to use your math and physics skills. You'd also **acquire** some really useful new skills and an in-depth **understanding** of the field.

Ada: Okay, but I'm not sure if that would be for me. An engineering major would be very **academic**. I wonder if I should try something more **vocational**. I actually like manual work better. I'd rather make something than write about it! Is it possible to do both? Maybe I could do an **internship** at an engineering company and then study after I see how the internship goes.

Advisor: Of course, you should consider an internship, but it would be helpful to take some engineering courses too. Have you done much research on different courses that are available?

Ada: Not yet.

Advisor: I suggest that you try to find out more about engineering courses. I could give you the names of some professors who teach the introductory engineering courses. You could talk to them and maybe even visit one of their classes.

Ada: Yes, that's a good idea. I think I could do that. I'd like to know more about what engineers actually do, and I'd rather talk to someone than just read the information on websites. Thanks.

Advisor: In that case, have you considered talking to some engineers about their work?

Ada: I don't know any engineers.

Advisor: Well, there are several engineering companies that will be at the college career fair next week. You should definitely attend that. Also, I know that some graduates from our engineering department will be attending the career fair as well. I'm sure we could arrange for you to talk with them. You could ask them what their jobs are like.

Ada: That would be great. I really want to know how hands-on engineering work is. I wouldn't mind the academic side of engineering, the math and the physics, but I think I'd really enjoy the actual work of engineering – you know, designing and making things. Computer engineering could be really interesting.

Advisor: You might want to try contacting a computer engineering company here in the city, then. In fact, I could help you with that. We could probably arrange a visit for you.

Ada: That would be fantastic. Thank you.

🔊 2.2

See script on page 42.

1 You're considering going to college, aren't you?
2 I like biology, so I really want to be a doctor.
3 You should consider the courses you like and the courses you do well in when choosing a major.
4 I'm considering studying art history.
5 I've always been interested in the way things work.
6 I think I could do that.
7 I wouldn't mind the academic side of biology.
8 ... but I might enjoy the practical side of linguistics.

🔊 2.4

Medical student: Hey, Adam. Come in. Sit down. Want something to drink?

Adam: No, thanks, I'm OK.

Medical student: Have you thought about the **medical** courses I suggested? I loved them when I was an undergrad.

Adam: A little. I've done a little research, but I'm having a hard time deciding what I want to do.

Medical student: That's understandable. There's a lot to think about. Is studying medicine the most important consideration for you?

Adam: Yes and no. The most important thing is probably that I do a medical program of some kind, but not necessarily one that involves a lot of study.

Medical student: OK.

Adam: Getting a **secure** job after I finish my program is important, though, and I really want to help people.

Medical student: What about location? Do you care about where you study?

Adam: Not really. That's probably the least important factor.

Medical student: OK, good. Well, I think we're getting somewhere. You get better grades than I ever did; you should consider studying to become a doctor.

Adam: I'm not sure about that.

Medical student: Really? Why not?

Adam: Well, I guess another one of my criteria is that the job is very **practical**.

Medical student: Sorry, but I have to disagree. I think being a doctor is a very practical job!

Adam: Yes, but I'd rather not have to study for so many years.

Medical student: Maybe you should consider becoming an emergency room nurse.

Adam: I've looked into that.

Medical student: You don't sound too interested in that idea. What else are you considering?

Adam: It depends. I'm not sure what I can apply for. There are a few programs where you can study to become an emergency medical technician – an EMT. They're the people who work on ambulances, assessing patients' conditions, performing emergency procedures, like applying **manual** pressure on someone's wounds after an accident. It also requires some **technical** knowledge of ambulance equipment. It's **professional** and practical.

Medical student: That's a tough job. Exciting, but tough, and very **physical**.

Adam: Yes, but it seems like a great way to really help people when they need it.

Medical student: So, what's the difference between the two programs?

Adam: The EMT program is very practical. When you work in an ambulance, you need a lot of practical skills to help people. You have to be very independent and confident to make decisions on your own, and of course there's the driver training too!

Medical student: OK, I see your point.

Adam: The emergency room nursing program is also practical, but it includes more theoretical work. Especially when you study the core subjects – learning about the human body and about medicine, and so on. It would involve a lot more **complex** study. You have to work closely with hospital staff. It's a degree program.

Medical student: And the EMT program?

Adam: It's a certificate program. So, it would take a lot less time, and I'd be able to start work quickly. It would be great to actually work after so much study. I've been studying my whole life. I'm ready to *do* something, have some adventures, so I'm not too sure about nursing.

Medical student: Yes, I can see that. Continuing on for more schooling like me isn't for everyone. It may not be the ideal program.

Adam: EMTs need in-depth understanding of how to deal with emergencies, and they need the ability to make quick decisions.

Medical student: I think you'd be good at it.

Adam: And if I wanted to continue my training, after working as a basic EMT, I could study to become an EMT specialist. That's another certificate program.

Medical student: But wouldn't you rather study to be a nurse? I imagine the pay would be better.

Adam: You're probably right, but I don't think it's for me.

Medical student: Why don't you get some more information about EMT programs, then, and find out which schools offer that certification.

Adam: That's a great idea.

Medical student: I guess you've made a decision, then. You're going to not follow in my footsteps and instead you'll apply for EMT training.

Adam: I think that's really what I want to do.

🔊 2.5

A: I think the most important factor is probably financial need.

B: I'm not sure about that. What if we say that financial need is number two?

C: So, what's number one?

B: I feel it's important to really focus on the applicants' potential contribution to society.

C: I think that's right. Why don't we rank the proposed courses of study according to their contribution to society?

A: OK, I can see your point, but why don't we just say that the interview is number one and financial need is number two?

C/D OK.

B: Wait a minute. I don't agree with that at all. Academic ability is much more important. What if we say that GPA, or grade point average, is the most important factor?

A: I think the rest of us are in agreement about the most important factors.

D: Well, I think the least important thing is the student's written application.

C: Sorry, I don't think I agree. They need to be able to write well.

B: Wait! Have you considered looking at the applicant's family situation?

🔊 2.6

1 **A:** Students need to be good at both writing and speaking.

B: I see. That's understandable.

2 **A:** Hotel workers are important, but emergency medical technicians save lives.

B: OK, I see your point.

3 **A:** The Chinese language is becoming more important all the time.

B: You might be right about that.

4 **A:** Why don't we say emergency medical technicians have the most important job?

B: OK, I think we all can agree with that.

5 **A:** Do we all agree that financial need is the most important factor?

B: Yes. We've made a decision.

6 **A:** Can we agree that grade point average is the most important factor?

B: I think we've come to an agreement.

🔊 2.7

Instructor: Hi, and welcome to Western University! Now, you all come from different countries and educational backgrounds, so I'm going to explain some important terms that you need to understand before you sign up for your classes. First of all: credits. Every class carries a certain number of credits. Most classes count for three credits, but some count for two, or four. In order to graduate you'll need to take about 120 credits in total, over four years. For most people, that will translate to between 12 and 15 credits per semester.

Student 1: I'm sorry, can you please say that again? How many credits do we need to take per semester?

Instructor: Most people take between 12 and 15 credits per semester.

Student 2: May I ask a question?

Instructor: Of course!

Student 2: Somebody told me that a three-credit class means three hours of class a week. Is that correct?

Instructor: Yes, that's more or less correct.

Student 2: So in other words, if I'm taking 15 credits, that's about 15 hours of class?

Instructor: Correct. And remember … you can sometimes get credit for work you have done outside college.

Student 1: Can you give us an example?

Instructor: For example, if you have taken an honors-level class in high school.

Student 1: I see …

Student 3: Could I ask about grades? What system do you use?

Instructor: We use a letter system. *A* is the highest grade. An *A* is 90% or higher. A *B* is 80 to 89% percent. A *C* is 70 to 79%. And a D is 65 to 69%. At this school, you need a *C* or better to pass a class. Some teachers do it differently, but that's the most common system.

Student 4: Can you explain the term *GPA*? I hear it a lot but I don't know what it means.

Instructor: *GPA* stands for Grade Point Average. You get four points for an *A*, three points for a *B*, two points for a *C*, and one point for a *D*. Your GPA is the average of all of your points.

Student 4: Thank you.

UNIT 3

▶ Corporate Wellness

Donna Sharples: My entire life my weight has been an issue. It's been an up-and-down battle.

Elaine Quijano (reporter): Less than two years ago 46-year-old Donna Sharples weighed 275 pounds and suffered from some serious health problems. But for this New Jersey businesswoman, the spark to better health came from her employer, the PHH Corporation. It pays workers up to $1,000 a year to make measurable improvements to their health.

Donna Sharples: I didn't think I'd gain any other benefit out of it, but the chance to earn extra cash was a motivating factor for me, absolutely.

Elaine Quijano: It's called incentive-based health care.

Adele Barbato: It is a win-win.

Elaine Quijano: Chief Human Resources Officer Adele Barbato says the program benefits the workers and the company. As employees get healthier, medical costs go down.

Adele Barbato: So we have less claims costs. We have less sick time, higher productivity, more engaged employees because they're feeling good about taking control of their wellness.

Elaine Quijano: And it really works. For every dollar a company spends on a corporate wellness program, there is a three- to six-dollar return on investment. At this company, the path to wellness starts with a few simple steps, literally.

Donna Sharples: Here's my pedometer.

Elaine Quijano: Everyone in the program gets a pedometer like this one, and every step is counted. The more you walk, the more money you get.

Donna Sharples: In the beginning, I was lucky if I could walk for five minutes straight on a treadmill, honestly, when I first started coming up here. But I just stuck with it and each day tried to add a little more time to it and increased it as much as I could.

Elaine Quijano: Keeping track of your progress is simple. Just plug the pedometer into your PC.

Donna Sharples: To date I've taken four million, thirteen thousand, eight hundred steps.

Elaine Quijano: Employees can also earn credit for being active in other ways, like this cardio class at the on-site gym, in the middle of the work day. And the focus on wellness extends to the cafeteria, which offers fresh, healthy choices. For Donna Sharples, the program has done much more than earn her extra cash and make her healthier. It's transformed her in a more fundamental way, one step at a time. Elaine Quijano, CBS News, New York.

🔊 **3.1**

Teacher: Throughout history, there have been many pandemics around the world: measles, malaria, cholera, the flu. So how does a common disease turn from an **outbreak** into a pandemic? Any ideas?

Student 1: People's general health and how close they live to each other can be major **factors** in the spread of disease, can't they?

Student 2: Yeah, so governments need to make sure people are in good health and live in good conditions to stop diseases from spreading.

Teacher: Well, that's a good idea, but there's a limit to what governments can do, especially in times of economic difficulty.

Student 2: And governments don't always have the power to say exactly how everyone should live.

Teacher: So what factors do you think would make a country at a high risk for a pandemic?

Student 3: Well, countries with large populations are probably at risk, especially where large numbers of people live close together.

Student 1: And countries where a lot of international travelers pass through, like the U.K. and other countries in dark and medium blue on the map.

Teacher: That's right. The countries most at risk of a pandemic these days are wealthier countries like the U.K., South Korea, the Netherlands, and Germany. What do those countries have in common?

Student 2: They're not all large countries, but they do all have large cities with big populations.

Student 1: And they're all places where a lot of international travelers might go. They have a lot of airports and potentially thousands of people coming in every day, from all over the world.

Teacher: Correct. If you look at those countries in light blue, they're at a medium or low risk for a pandemic because they have less dense populations, less international travel, fewer borders, etc. OK, so imagine you're an advisor to your government.

You want to protect your country from a pandemic. What should you do?

Student 1: You should give everyone a vaccine.

Teacher: A vaccine. OK, good idea. Can anyone explain what that is?

Student 2: It's a kind of medicine, isn't it?

Teacher: Yes, sort of. Most medicines are given to patients after they have the illness, to help them **recover**, but a vaccine is different. A vaccine provides disease **prevention**. If people get the flu vaccine, they often don't become **infected**. So if we wanted to avoid pandemics, then governments would need to implement vaccination programs for common diseases, wouldn't they?

Student 3: The government should force everyone to have vaccines. They should give a vaccine to people as soon as an outbreak **occurs** because prevention is generally much easier than **treatment**. When governments focus on the prevention of disease, pandemics become very rare.

Student 2: I'm not sure I agree. The trouble is, organisms that cause disease, like bacteria or viruses, change every year. So a vaccine that worked really well last year may not be effective this year.

Student 1: There's another thing to consider too; a lot of people don't want to have a vaccine that might not work. The government can't force people to get a vaccine, can it?

Teacher: Well, I don't think any governments do, but in the event of a pandemic, they definitely encourage people to get it, and a lot of people do. People don't want to **contract** a disease, do they? So other than vaccination, what other ways are there of stopping the spread of disease?

Student 1: International travel is a big risk to a disease spreading quickly. We shouldn't allow people with diseases into the country.

Student 3: I'm not sure I agree. The trouble is most people spread diseases before they even know they have them.

Student 2: And there's another problem. How could people prove whether or not they have diseases? It would be impossible to set up a system for checking it.

Student 1: During a pandemic, we should stop all flights from countries that are affected, shouldn't we? If we don't let people into the country, then the disease won't get here.

Student 2: But there's another side to that argument. People travel all the time for business. It would have a terrible effect on the economy, wouldn't it?

Student 3: But also, in most countries, people who live near the border travel back and forth, sometimes every day. If countries stopped people from traveling, a lot of people could lose their jobs. It could also separate families.

Teacher: Well, those are some really interesting views from all of you. Can anyone think of some simpler suggestions for decreasing the risk of pandemics, then? Perhaps not as large scale as closing down country borders?

Student 1: Well, people who have the flu should stay home from school or from work, shouldn't they?

🔊 **3.2**

1 A lot of people don't want to have a vaccine that might not work. The government can't force people to get a vaccine, can it?

2 During a pandemic, we should stop all flights from countries that are affected, shouldn't we?

3 People travel all the time for business. It would have a terrible effect on the economy, wouldn't it?

🔊 **3.3**

1 So this is a very serious disease, isn't it?

2 So this is a very serious disease, isn't it?

3 It's a kind of medicine, isn't it?

4 Governments need to implement vaccination programs for common diseases, don't they?

5 The government can't force people to get a vaccine, can it?

6 People don't want to contract a disease, do they?

7 During a pandemic, we should stop all flights from countries that are affected, shouldn't we?

8 People who have the flu should stay home from school or from work, shouldn't they?

🔊 **3.4**

Host: Flu season is here, but experts and the public are divided on the subject of vaccination. Those in favor of the flu vaccine say that it may help you avoid getting sick and may also help stop the spread of the disease. They point out that this may save lives. Those experts against the flu vaccine argue that there is no proof that it works. Some go so far as to say that it may be unsafe because it is produced very quickly, though there is no evidence to support this claim. The fact is that there is no research or **clinical** evidence to show that either side is correct. As the debate continues, statistics show that only about 30% of us choose to get the flu vaccine each year.

🔊 3.5

Host: Since the news that this year's flu vaccine is ready, the government has advised that the old, young, and people with medical problems be vaccinated. However, not everyone thinks vaccination is a good idea. According to the Centers for Disease Control and Prevention, less than 50% of those eligible to get the flu vaccine – most people except for the very young and very old – got the flu vaccine as a **precaution** last year. That means over 50% did not get vaccinated. Of that 50%, some are actively against the flu vaccine.

In today's debate, we'll begin with flu expert Dr. Sandra Smith, who is in favor of flu vaccination. After that, we'll hear from alternative medicine practitioner Mr. Mark Li, who is against flu vaccination.

Dr. Smith will now begin. Dr. Smith?

Dr. Smith: Thank you. Well, influenza, or the flu, is a respiratory disease that can make you feel extremely sick. Most people who get the flu recover after several days. While they may feel terrible, there are usually no long-lasting problems. However, the flu can cause severe illness or worse for a small percentage of the people who get it. It may not sound like a lot, but actually this is hundreds of thousands of people around the world each year. It can be especially serious for the very old and the very young. Obviously, we want to do everything in our power to stop the infection from spreading. This brings us to vaccination. When people get vaccinated, less flu can spread through the population.

Vaccines have saved millions of lives. They're a proven method of disease prevention. Scientists have been developing flu vaccines from the 1930s up to today, so we have a lot of experience with them. **Researchers** make new flu vaccines every year based on the previous year's flu virus. The World Health Organization recommends that children between the ages of six months and five years, people over 65, pregnant women, and anyone who already has a serious illness get the flu vaccine. They also recommend vaccinations for health-care workers. To finish up, let me say this: I'm a flu specialist.

I research the virus and work closely with flu patients all the time, so I'm constantly around the virus. I've gotten the vaccine. All of my colleagues have gotten the vaccine. None of us have caught the flu. If we hadn't gotten the vaccine, we could have caught the flu each year. There's no guarantee that vaccination will prevent you from getting the flu, but it won't hurt you, and there's a chance it could save your life. How would you feel if someone in your family did not get the vaccine and then became really sick?

Host: We'll now have the statement against vaccination from Mr. Mark Li.

Mr. Li: Thank you and thank you, Dr. Smith. Let me start by saying that I'm not against all vaccines. Dr. Smith is absolutely right that many vaccines work very well and that millions of lives have been saved by vaccination. There's plenty of good **scientific data** that **proves** that. If scientists hadn't developed the polio vaccine, the world would be very different today. But let me ask you this: has the flu vaccine been properly tested? Have there been proper clinical **trials** to prove that it works, that it stops infection? Does it really provide prevention of the disease?

For most medicines, the government makes sure that proper tests are carried out, but this isn't the case with the flu vaccine. There isn't one single scientific study that proves that this year's flu vaccine works. The packaging on this flu vaccine clearly states that "No **controlled** trials have been performed that demonstrate that this vaccine causes a reduction in influenza." It's here in black and white.

If it says on the package that there's no proof that it's an effective prevention, why are we using it? Yes, vaccination can be good, but flu vaccination is just a big experiment, and it may actually be doing more harm than good. If it were proven, then I would consider it.

Host: Thank you, Mr. Li. Dr. Smith, do you have anything to add?

Dr. Smith: Thank you. You have some interesting points, Mr. Li. It's true that when the flu emerges every year, it's a bit different than the year before. When making a vaccine, researchers have to try to figure out how the flu is going to change and adjust it to the new virus. If we waited until the new virus emerges, it would be too late.

So while Mr. Li is right – we don't do clinical trials of the flu vaccine in the way that we do trials for other medicines – that doesn't mean we aren't scientific in our methods. I'd definitely like to challenge the idea that there's no scientific basis for our work. I disagree with Mr. Li on that point. Let me tell you more about my work in that area.

We can prove in the laboratory that vaccines can reduce the risk of getting a disease, generally. What we don't know is exactly how this year's flu virus will change, but we can use our experience to make a prediction. As for the question of the vaccine being dangerous: it doesn't contain a live virus, so you definitely can't get the flu from the vaccine. If people are vaccinated and then happen to become sick, that doesn't logically mean the vaccine caused the illness. They were most likely around the virus before they were vaccinated.

Mr. Li: Well, I'm sure Dr. Smith is a very good doctor, but I think the flu vaccine package I mentioned earlier is clear. It's obvious that the vaccine hasn't been properly tested.

The other big concern, of course, is safety. A lot of us believe that the vaccine actually causes people to get sick rather than making them well – so she and I disagree on that point. I'm talking about side effects. Some people have gotten really sick after being vaccinated. This can be anything from headaches to stomach problems. Do you really want to use a medication that might make you sick? Supposing you gave your kids the vaccine and it made them worse rather than better? Some people also believe that the vaccine may give you the flu rather than stopping you from catching it. I've had patients who were healthy, then got the flu vaccine and got sick. Medicines shouldn't make us sick. That's why I'm against the flu vaccine, and that's why I don't think anyone at all should have it.

Host: Thank you both.

🔊 **3.6**

1 Affordable health care is an issue for poor people all over the world, and not just in developing countries. In his book, *Pathologies of Power*, published by University of California Press in 2003, Dr. Paul Farmer points out that poor people in some prosperous American cities have a lower life expectancy than people in China or India.

2 Heart disease is a leading cause of death in the United States. According to statistics from the Centers for Disease Control and Prevention, more than 600,000 Americans die of heart disease each year. That's one in every four deaths in this country.

3 Doctors are making progress in fighting cancer. A 2016 report by Rebecca Siegel and her colleagues at the American Cancer Society found that the death rate from cancer has dropped by 23% since 1991.

UNIT 4

▶ Cloning Endangered Species

Reporter: They are called bantengs, and although one of the week-old calves just died, the fact that they were born at all could put scientists one step closer to saving some endangered species. The animals were cloned from the frozen skin cells of a banteng which died 23 years ago.

Man: I'm rather still astounded by the fact that you can take the nucleus of a cell and produce a living animal.

Reporter: It's called *nuclear cell transfer*, injecting the banteng's genetic material into the egg of a living cow. It's been done before with an endangered animal called a gaur. It died in just two days. The banteng was euthanized after developing complications from the cloning. While the news of the birth is astonishing, it also worries some conservationists.

Conservationist: If you don't deal with protecting habitat and dealing with all the root causes of endangerment, it doesn't matter how many animals you are able to produce in the lab and try to sort of fling back into the wild, they're going to face the same fate as their wild counterparts.

Reporter: The scientists at Advanced Cell Technology in Massachusetts, where both the banteng and gaur were cloned, agree to some extent.

Scientist: However, it doesn't make much sense to preserve the habitat if you don't have any animals to preserve.

Reporter: If you're wondering, "Can this technology be used to clone extinct animals like the mammoth," hold on. Since cloning needs preserved animal tissue, bringing back the dinosaurs remains the stuff of science fiction, for now.

🔊 **4.1**

Planet Earth is dynamic and always changing. Just 10,000 years ago, about half of the planet was covered in ice, but before that period, the Earth had been very steamy and warm, with vast forests and large bodies of water. It may surprise you that oceans had covered the whole planet until about 2.5 billion years ago, when land formed above sea level. As you can see, the Earth has experienced quite a lot of environmental change.

Today only about 10% of the planet is covered in ice, as the Earth has been warming since the last ice age. Part of this environmental change is due to natural, rather than human, causes.

Sometimes, natural forces can destroy the environment. In 1991, a volcano in the Philippines erupted and killed many people and animals. It destroyed around 300 square miles of farmland and a huge area of forest. It also caused severe floods when rivers were blocked with volcanic ash.

However, humans are also responsible for a lot of habitat destruction. There were originally more than 6 million square miles of rainforest worldwide. Less than three and a half million remain today, and deforestation is occurring at a rate of approximately 1,722,225 square feet per year. In Europe, only about 15% of land hasn't been **modified** by humans.

In some places, **habitats** haven't been destroyed, but they have been broken into parts, for example, separated by roads. This is called fragmentation. If animals are used to moving around throughout the year and a road is built through the middle of their habitat, fragmentation can cause serious problems.

Humans haven't only affected the land and its animals; they have also affected the sea. Pollution from **coastal** cities has damaged the ocean environment and destroyed the habitat of fish and other sea life.

Habitat destruction hasn't been bad news for all animals. In fact, some species have **adapted** extremely well to living closely with people and benefit from living near them.

In Africa and Asia, monkeys live in cities alongside people and **exploit** the human environment by stealing food or eating things that humans have thrown away. In Singapore, the 1,500 wild monkeys that live in and around the city have become a tourist attraction. In North America, coyotes have wandered into urban areas, even big cities like San Francisco and Chicago. Coyotes have learned to cross busy roads safely to find places to live in the city without being noticed. They survive by eating a wide variety of things, such as gophers, squirrels, and rabbits, but not everyone welcomes the coyotes. They sometimes eat people's dogs and cats and might attack pet owners if they try to defend their dogs or cats. Likewise, police in India recently spotted several young leopards in the streets of Mumbai. The leopards had moved into the city from the nearby forests. One expert said that the surprising thing was that leopards had been in the city

for a long time, but people rarely saw them. Leopards are very secretive, and they prefer not to be seen.

One other animal that is as at home in both the city and in the countryside is the raccoon. In fact, raccoons are so at home in the city that the number of city raccoons has increased. Raccoons have different diets depending on their environment. Common foods include fruit, plants, nuts, and rodents. Raccoons living in the city eat garbage.

We tend to think of human activity as always having a negative **impact** on the environment. However, some people feel that we can have a positive impact, too. **Conservation** means trying to save habitats. Ecotourism is an approach to travel and vacations where people visit natural areas such as rainforests, except rather than destroy the environment, they help preserve it. Visitors to the La Selva Amazon Eco Lodge in Ecuador watch and learn about local wildlife, visit tribes who live in the forest, and stay in an environmentally friendly hotel. Their presence doesn't damage the local environment, and most guests leave the hotel as conservationists. When they experience the beauty of nature firsthand, they feel strongly that they want to protect and preserve it.

Not everyone feels that ecotourism is actually helping the environment. Tourists who travel long distances by airplane create pollution, as do resorts, which use local resources such as fresh water and produce **waste** that creates pollution in the local environment.

🔊 4.2

See script on page 88.

🔊 4.3

Before she wrote her influential book *Silent Spring* in 1962, Rachel Carson had spent years working for the U.S. government at environmental agencies like the U.S. Bureau of Fisheries and the U.S. Fish and Wildlife Service. During her time there, she did her own personal research and writing. By 1955, Carson had already published several books on environmental research when she began to do research full-time. One subject that she was particularly interested in was the effects of pesticides on the environment and on human health. During World War II, the government used the pesticide DDT to protect people against diseases caused by pests. After the war, farmers sprayed large amounts of DDT into the air to protect their crops. Carson had heard that the chemical was making people sick with cancer and was causing other animals to die, so she decided to do scientific research on the subject and publish it as a book to warn people about the risks. After Carson released *Silent Spring*, the pesticide industry attacked her for her research. However, the U.S. government responded by banning the use of DDT in the United States. Soon her book was translated into several languages and was published around the world.

🔊 4.4

The topic of my talk is the decline and destruction of the world's deserts. First, I'm going to talk about the desert environment and wildlife. Then we'll look at the threats to this environment. Finally, we'll talk about what is being done to save the world's deserts.

Let's begin by looking at some background information from the United Nations Environment Programme. The United Nations reports in *Global Deserts Outlook* that the Earth's deserts cover about 13 million square miles, or about 25% of the Earth's surface. Deserts are home to 560 million people, or about 8% of the world's population, but as I'll explain, people all over the world rely on things that come from this environment.

Humans have learned to exploit the resources of the desert for survival and profit by adapting their behavior, culture, and technology to this **harsh** environment. To give you an example, tribes such as the Topnaar in southwestern Africa are known for their ability to survive in deserts due to their use of local plants and animals for food, medicine, and clothing. They have an understanding of the natural world. The Bedouins, who live from North Africa to the Syrian deserts, are skilled at using animals to provide transportation, food, and clothing and also at growing basic foods around desert rivers. The Topnaar and the Bedouins are just two examples of people who live in and rely on the desert environment for the things they need. However, city dwellers benefit from the desert, too.

Certain **minerals** are found in deserts, which provide a large portion of the world's **diamonds**, as well as **copper**, gold, and other metals. Deserts are a major source of oil and **natural gas**, too. These desert products are used by industries and people all over the world every day. Until these natural resources were discovered, of course, changes to desert habitats had not really affected people very much. But what I'm saying is that nowadays, even though most people may not live in a desert, we actually are all affected by these kinds of environmental changes, even if we live in cities.

Agricultural products are also grown in deserts and exported around the world. Because their climates are warm and their land tends to be inexpensive, desert countries are able to grow and sell food all year. A good example of this is Egyptian cotton. New methods of irrigation are being developed so that desert agricultural systems can use water more efficiently. So we can see that deserts are important, not only for the people who live in them, but for everyone who uses products that come from a desert environment. That's all I have to say on that point.

Moving on to the typical desert environment. In summer, the ground surface temperature in most deserts reaches 175 degrees Fahrenheit (80 degrees Celsius), and there is very little rain. Despite these harsh conditions, a wide variety of plants and animals live in and are supported by this environment. For example, there are reportedly over 2,200 different plant species in the desert regions of Saudi Arabia, based on research from King Saud University.

Small plants are especially important in a desert environment because they hold the soil in place, which allows larger plants to grow. Acacia trees can grow well in extremely hot, dry conditions, but its seeds need stable soil to begin growing. Smaller plants, therefore, help the larger ones, and in this way, all desert plants help hold the dry soil in place, which helps reduce dust storms.

Deserts are also an important animal habitat. One of the best known desert animals in the Arabian Peninsula is the Arabian oryx, which weighs about 150 pounds (68 kilograms) and is about three feet tall — that's almost a meter. It rests during the heat of the day and searches for food and water when temperatures are cooler. Experts say that the oryx can sense rain and move towards it.

These examples show that the desert is an ecosystem that supports a variety of important plant and animal life. The problem is that human activity is affecting modern deserts. According to the United Nations, traditional ways of life are changing as human activities such as cattle ranching, farming, and large-scale tourism grow. The process of bringing water into the desert to grow plants is making the soil too salty. The construction of dams for power generation and water supply and an increase in **mining** have also begun to have a greater impact on the desert. Owing to the destruction of desert plants, dust storms are more common, and desert animals, therefore, have less food to eat. Data from the United Nations shows that every year, nearly 2% of healthy desert disappears. Today, more than 50% of the world's desert habitats are **wilderness** areas, but by 2050, it may be as low as 31%.

If we lose the world's deserts, we lose everything I spoke about in the first part of my talk. The Topnaar and Bedouin way of life will certainly disappear, but what does this mean for the rest of the world? Well, everyone on Earth will experience an increase of dust and dirt in the air as desert plants die. If desert soil becomes too salty to grow plants, we'll also lose a valuable source of food, and I'm talking about foods that we all eat. If we allow deserts to be destroyed, life all over Earth will change. To put it another way, we will all be affected. Now, the big question is, what is being done about the destruction of deserts?

The United Nations Environment Programme offers two main solutions. First, we can begin to manage desert resources carefully, instead of abusing them. This means using the desert for things we need, as well as not damaging it further. It would mean carefully controlling the way we use water. Secondly, we can apply technological solutions. The UN gives the example of using the latest computer technology to help forecast how climate change will affect deserts and using that information to prepare for these changes. We can also make better use of two resources freely available in the desert: the wind and the sun. These can be used to provide clean energy on a fairly small scale within existing desert cities. According to the blog *A Smarter Planet*, scientists in Saudi Arabia are already using solar energy to produce fresh water in the desert for agricultural use.

To summarize, deserts are not only important to the people who live in them, but to plants, animals, and people everywhere, from the Bedouin tribes to city dwellers. Human activity is causing the destruction of desert habitats, but there are ways in which we can help stop this.

🔊 4.5

Anchor: Are you a procrastinator? Do you often put off doing your work, your homework, or your assignments for your classes? Well, you are not alone. A recent survey of 1,300 high school and college students found that approximately 87% of high school and college students regularly avoid or postpone schoolwork. Almost half of the students that procrastinate – 45% – said that procrastination often has a bad effect on their grades.

The report found that male and female students procrastinate for slightly different reasons. Male students are more likely to say that they don't like doing schoolwork and they would rather be doing something else. Female students are more likely to say they feel overwhelmed – they have so much to do that they don't know where to start.

So what are students doing instead of studying? The answer is not a surprise. For both males and females, the most common ways of avoiding schoolwork were watching movies or TV and using social media.

Here in our studio we have Mercedes Kaufman, who is a student advisor at Western University. Mercedes, does any of this information surprise you?

Kaufman: No. Procrastination is a huge problem among college students, both male and female – particularly younger students who are coming straight from high school.

Anchor: And do you think that social media has an effect on this?

Kaufman: Yes, I think so. There are so many distractions, and it's so easy to spend an hour playing a game on your phone or looking at social media. Students really need to learn how to manage their time.

Anchor: Can you give us an example of some strategies that students could use?

Kaufman: Well, we train students to organize their time by using planners and to-do lists. We show them how to divide up the work they have to do and see how they can do things a bit at a time. We also teach them to plan their work at the time of day when they are likely to be most productive.

Anchor: Thank you, Mercedes. Now we'd like to hear from our listeners. What strategies do you use to avoid procrastinating? Give us a call at 905 …

UNIT 5

▶ The Skyscraper

New York City may have made them famous, but skyscrapers were born in Chicago, Illinois. A terrible fire in 1871 made it possible for architects to experiment with new building techniques that would allow them to make buildings taller than ever before. These stately brown stone buildings are some of the world's first skyscrapers.

Louis Sullivan, known as the father of the skyscraper, lived and worked in Chicago. This is his Auditorium Building on Michigan Avenue, completed in 1889.

Sullivan believed that the new social and economic strength of the United States required a new architecture. And his idea that tall buildings represent power is still popular 125 years later.

Sullivan described the skyscraper as the perfect symbol of the proud spirit of the American man. But it was really the symbol of the proud American businessman. By 1920, there were over 300,000 corporations in the United States, serving 100 million consumers in an enormous single market – it was the biggest, most powerful economy the world had ever seen.

Above all, skyscrapers represented American corporate success. They changed the appearance of American cities. The skylines of New York and Chicago looked like bar charts or graphs, with the tallest buildings representing the richest, most powerful companies. And the same is still true in cities around the world today – from Dubai to Shanghai, from Seoul to Kuala Lumpur.

🔊 5.1

Alan: Khalid, we need to talk about that warehouse the company plans to **obtain** in Westside.

Khalid: OK. I've just seen the pictures. I think there's a lot of **potential** there.

Alan: Really? I'm afraid we might be biting off more than we can chew.

Khalid: Really? Why?

Alan: First, the problem is the Westside area itself. Thirty years ago, it was a thriving industrial neighborhood with a lot of businesses. Now, it's a half-empty wasteland. It's ugly. There are lots of abandoned buildings, and the area isn't really used for anything. No one wants to go there. Second, the warehouse we're looking at is in terrible condition. It was abandoned about 20 years ago. It's beginning to sink into the ground, and it's falling apart – we would need to do some serious work to bring the building back to good condition Acquiring such an old building could be a huge mistake.

Khalid: Really? I think the project is going to be a great success. In fact, I think it's a potential goldmine.

Alan: Um, OK. Could you expand on that?

Khalid: There's been a lot of activity in Westside recently. There is development and restoration going on nearby, and I think it's really going to **transform** the area. Westside is becoming popular with people who work in the financial district, which is close by. Rent is still low there, and a new restaurant opens almost every week. I **anticipate** the neighborhood becoming really trendy. No one has spent much money there in the past 20 years, but **investment** in the area has increased in the past year. We're going to see a lot more improvement as well.

Alan: That may be true, but that building is more like a prison than a potential shopping mall. People would never want to go shopping there. I think the first thing we'd need to do would be tear it down, and that would cost us a lot of money.

Khalid: Have you considered doing work on the building instead of tearing it down? It has some beautiful original **features**.

Alan: It looks like it's probably going to **collapse**!

Khalid: I'm not sure it's that bad. I think the original building has a lot of potential.

Alan: I think we really want to transform the area with something modern. Why not just start over and build a new building?

Khalid: If we designed it properly, we could maintain the old architectural features, such as the red bricks and the stone. Those construction materials would better match the style of some of the other buildings around it. It would reflect the character of the area. We are going to give the old building a new lease on life.

Alan: Maybe, but I think it would be better to transform the area with an architectural landmark, something new and **contemporary**. It would be more of a transformation if we built a modern building made of materials like steel and glass.

Khalid: Couldn't we do both? We'll maintain more of a connection to the past if we include the old building as part of the new one. We could rebuild the warehouse using red bricks similar to those in the original structure and construct a new glass and steel extension – adding on to the building rather than building a whole new building. It would also create more floor space that could be used for retail space. We'd have enough room for at least two or three stores there.

Alan: I hadn't thought of doing it that way.

Khalid: Another option to consider would be putting stores on the ground floor and apartments or offices above. If we added a floor or two to the top of the building, we could definitely use glass and steel for that.

Alan: Would they be luxury apartments?

Khalid: Maybe. We could have a modern, urban, or city-like design using the old architectural materials and features.

Alan: Such as?

Khalid: We could keep some of the original features as they are, such as the long and heavy pieces of wood used to support the ceilings and the inside of the red brick supporting walls that help support the roof. They would then become a decorative feature.

Alan: So not traditional apartments at all, then?

Khalid: No, not at all. Very modern.

Alan: It's an expensive plan, and not everyone will like it.

Khalid: We wouldn't be the first to do this sort of thing, though. We can look at some other examples around the city where the same thing has been done successfully, if you're interested in the idea.

Alan: If we make that the first phase of our planning process, we can make a better decision about how to balance the traditional and modern features of the project before we go on to the design and building phases.

Khalid: There's probably a Westside neighborhood association or business association. We could meet with them and get their views.

Alan: You're right. We really should speak to some businesspeople in the area and arrange to take a better look at the building.

Khalid: Let's do it.

🔊 **5.2**

See script on page 109.

🔊 **5.3**

Jamal: Maria, John. Thanks for taking the time to meet with us.

Maria and John: No problem. / My pleasure.

Jamal: We have the first set of plans, and we think you'll be really pleased with what we've put together. After discussing a lot of options, we now anticipate building a single eight-story apartment building.

Tom: You can see from the pictures here that we are certainly going to fit this into the area by using part of the wasteland, the large area of land that hasn't been developed behind the current housing area.

Jamal: One of the biggest benefits of this plan is that it will create housing for as many as 200 people.

Maria: I can't quite tell from the drawing … what materials are you going to use?

Tom: The outside is made of glass and steel.

John: And what's the cost of this plan?

Jamal: Around eight million dollars.

Maria: Eight million? Wow. The plan is definitely **ambitious**!

Jamal: Yes, we're aware that it's over the construction budget of 7.5 million, but we are going to review the budget in light of some of our suggestions.

Maria: Well, I have to say, we weren't expecting the building to be so tall.

John: Exactly. The **existing** buildings in the neighborhood are no higher than two stories, and you've placed the new building very close to them. I'm **concerned** about the other buildings on the site. The plan would block daylight for existing homes. We're probably going to get a lot of complaints from the current residents.

Jamal: We could consider using reflective glass instead, then. You know, like a mirror. It's used in big cities to give a feeling of open sky.

Maria: That's a great idea, but I'm not sure it addresses the main problem. The real issue here is the height of the building. I strongly recommend that you reconsider this. After all, we originally suggested housing for about 100 people.

Tom: Yes, we've doubled that.

Maria: OK. Would you mind telling us a bit more about why you decided that?

Jamal: Well, our thinking was that this would increase your company's income from the building because you could sell or rent more apartments.

John: We thought that might be an option at first, too, but now we realize it won't work. We have to think about the houses that are already in the area. We really need to consider how the new building will contribute to the look of the area – that is, how it will fit in with the other buildings.

Tom: When you say "fit in," do you mean we should copy the style of existing buildings?

John: No. We don't expect you to copy, but we also don't want to completely transform the feeling of the area either. So by "fit in," I mean that it should look as though it belongs there. Our original suggestion was that the building should reflect the size and materials of the other buildings in the area.

Tom: OK, I see what you mean.

John: I have one other concern. You described the natural area you'd like to build on as "wasteland," but actually, those are woods. The kids who already live in the area play there, and we want to maintain that open, natural area with all the trees. The residents really value having access to nature nearby.

Maria: Exactly.

John: As it stands, this plan with the tall, single building and the loss of the natural space would be very **controversial**. Wouldn't it be better if we used the first design you supplied to identify a few priorities?

Jamal: Yes, that's a good idea.

Maria: OK ... first, we need to think about what will be **appropriate** with the existing houses. What about more smaller, shorter buildings? We could have four two-story buildings and, following our original plan, try to house 100 rather than 200 people. That might be better.

John: And while we like the idea of contemporary design, I'm not sure glass and steel is appropriate. Lots of glass is a great idea, but in my view, the only viable option is to use brick, like the existing buildings.

Tom: OK. So we're talking about four two-storey brick buildings that can house about 25 people each?

John: Right.

Tom: That seems like an obvious solution, but it doesn't address the issue of cost.

John: What do you mean?

Tom: Well, four smaller buildings will cost more than one larger one.

John: Well, I guess we'll have to see the actual costs to discuss that. Are we going to consider three buildings?

Tom: Yes, that's a possibility.

Jamal: And you mentioned having **adequate** green space. We didn't realize children play in those woods. We need to be **sympathetic** to their needs, so we need to find a different solution. How about we position the new buildings near the edge of the woods?

Maria: Yes, that's possible. We can't acquire the land next to our site because it's public property, but we can benefit from being near that open space. The residents would definitely be able to enjoy the views then.

Tom: I like your thinking. I completely agree.

Jamal: OK, so I think we need to go back and start over again.

John: Yes, I think you're right. I'm sorry, I hope we didn't waste your time.

Jamal: Not at all. I think we understand the site a lot better now, and I feel confident we can come up with a good plan over the next two weeks.

🔊 5.4

See script on page 115.

🔊 5.5

See script on page 118.

🔊 5.6

Student 1: Keep up with your course work. In college, there's usually nobody to tell you to study, so it's easy to just put it off. But there are quizzes and tests all the time ... and reading ... and papers ... and you're supposed to do a lot of work on your own outside class. So you really can't wait until the end of the semester to study.

Student 2: When you choose your classes, don't just take classes your friends are taking ... or classes that you think are going to be easy. Take a class in a new subject ... maybe something that you don't know a lot about. It helps you to explore your interests and get to know the different fields of study that are out there. It might be your favorite class of the whole semester!

Student 3: It's really important to ask questions in class. Usually other people have the same question, so it helps the class. Professors also expect you to participate in group work and discussions, and you usually get a better grade when you do!

Student 4: Get to know your professors. Go see them during office hours when you have questions. It shows that you're interested, and they're usually happy to help you. If you have a good relationship with a professor in your field, you can learn a lot from them. Sometimes you can help them with their research.

UNIT 6

▶ Solar Panels at Home

Barry Mathis: You gotta back up a little bit, whoa.

Thalia Assuras (reporter): Meet Barry and Anita Mathis. Two kids ...

Barry Mathis: Give it to Mommy.

Thalia Assuras: Big new house ...

Barry Mathis: My favorite feature of the house is the curved staircase.

Thalia Assuras: And a tiny electric bill.

Anita Mathis: It was kind of mind-blowing when I first moved into this house because I would open power bills, and I would just start laughing. Because it just didn't make any sense that you could save this much money on electricity.

Thalia Assuras: It's not that the Mathises are energy sensitive. They have big appliances and, of course, air conditioning. The secret is on the roof. Look closely. Those shiny panels are solar energy pads.

Barry Mathis: You almost have to show people where the tiles are that are solar. If it had big space-invader stuff on top of the house, definitely would have been a problem for me.

Thalia Assuras: I've never done an interview on a roof before, I have to tell you. This is a solar revolution in the making. Solar panels are now relatively small, fit seamlessly into a roof, and shrink energy costs. Are these solar panels going to pay for the energy of this house?

Man: They're going to offset 70% of the consumption of this house.

Thalia Assuras: My bill is 70% less.

Man: Correct.

John Rawlston: As you see, we're still doing a lot of work in here.

Thalia Assuras: Developer John Rawlston has built 150 solar homes in California. All have this unique feature: they can make so much energy, they feed power to the electric company, literally making the meter spin backwards, reducing the bill. How's that possible?

John Rawlston: If you're creating more electricity than you're using, it will spin backwards, and it will actually reduce your total kilowatts.

Thalia Assuras: So I could get zero, couldn't I?

John Rawlston: You could have less than zero.

Thalia Assuras: You know the saying about a home's biggest selling point – it's all about location, location, location. Well, that's a major problem with this concept. Unless you live in a place like California with all this sunshine, it's just not practical. But builders claim that's going to change soon. They say these panels are so efficient they will be usable even in states with short days and less light.

John Rawlston: We are making electricity right now.

Thalia Assuras: Yeah, you can see it right here on the meter.

The state of California covers about half the cost, and local power companies are required to give homeowners credit for the power their house makes.

Barry Mathis: When we're away, we're making money.

Thalia Assuras: But don't think the Mathises spend any time watching their meter.

Barry Mathis: And that's really one of the pretty parts of the whole idea, is that this happens without us knowing anything about it. It's just there.

Thalia Assuras: They just enjoy the house, bask in the easy money, and let the sun do the work. In Roseville, California, I'm Thalia Assuras for *Eye on America*.

🔊 6.1

Reporter: This is Andrew Thompson, reporting from the Spanish island of El Hierro, about 250 miles (400 kilometers) off the coast of Africa. It's pretty far from Madrid, which is about 1,250 miles (2,000 kilometers) away. Today, we're going to talk to two of the 11,000 people who live here, to find out what's so special about the island. First, this is Pedro Rodriguez, who owns a seafood restaurant on the island. Hello, Pedro.

Pedro: Hello, Andrew.

Reporter: So, how long have you lived on El Hierro?

Pedro: I haven't lived here for very long. I came from Madrid about five years ago.

Reporter: Don't you like it here?

Pedro: I love it here! I wish I had come a lot sooner than I did. I spent most of my life in Madrid.

Reporter: City life can be tough. I suppose island life is rather more relaxing.

Pedro: Exactly. El Hierro is my home now.

Reporter: So, what's so great about El Hierro?

Pedro: In the city, everyone hurries everywhere. You are surrounded by traffic, and you never feel like you can really relax. What's more, my career was in banking, which is an especially stressful job.
I love the sound of the sea. I love the peace and quiet, and I feel free here. City life was never like that. When I was living in the city, I worked in banking, as I said. It paid well and I was able to buy my restaurant, but I should have left the city when I was a much younger man.

Reporter: So you love the quiet life on El Hierro, but is there anything else that makes El Hierro special?

Pedro: Well, for one thing, El Hierro is completely energy independent!

Reporter: Energy independent?

Pedro: Yes. In the past, the power on the island was provided by oil. A lot of money was paid to ship 40,000 barrels of oil over from the **mainland** every year. It cost the island over two million dollars a year. Now, all our energy is created right here on the island.

Reporter: And for more about that, we'll now talk to engineer Sofia Martinez.

Sofia: Hello, Andrew.

Reporter: I wonder if you could tell us about the way you **generate** energy here on El Hierro.

Sofia: Well, if you've spent a day or two here, you may have noticed we have a lot of wind.

Reporter: Yes. In fact, it's blowing pretty hard outside right now.

Sofia: Well, for about 3,000 hours, or for about 30% of the year, the wind here blows hard enough to turn wind turbines, which can provide electricity.

Reporter: Does El Hierro rely completely on wind to power the island?

Sofia: No. The island's wind turbines have a **capacity** of about 11 megawatts, about enough to power 3,500 homes, but it's only one **element**. The bigger problem is that the wind doesn't blow all the time, so the power source isn't **consistent**.

Reporter: So you need another energy source on windless days?

Sofia: That was the challenge: to create an energy generation system, or a **network** of systems, that could supply enough energy for the island all the time. And the solution was hydroelectric power.

Reporter: What is hydroelectric power exactly?

Sofia: Hydroelectric power is when energy is converted into another form, such as electricity. The initial source of this energy is from water.

Reporter: But doesn't hydroelectric power require a river and a dam? Isn't El Hierro too small for a river?

Sofia: A river with a dam is the usual way of producing hydroelectric power, but really, all you need is water that can move from a high place to a lower place to get energy from the water.

Reporter: OK …

Sofia: At the center of El Hierro is a dormant volcano – a volcano that is no longer active. In the middle of the volcano, we built a **reservoir** that holds over 17 million cubic feet (500,000 cubic meters) of water, at a height of 2,297 feet (700 meters) above sea level. So that's our water in a high place.

Reporter: But you don't get much rain here. What happens when all of the water runs out of the reservoir?

Sofia: Well, I mentioned the wind turbines. The wind power and the hydroelectric power are in a network together. When the wind is blowing, energy from the wind turbines pumps water up into the reservoir.

Reporter: So the wind turbines power the pumping station?

Sofia: Right. We also use the wind power for all of our electrical needs, when it blows. Then when the wind stops, we let water run out of the reservoir and through some turbines. The turbines turn generators and we have hydroelectric power we can access.

Reporter: So the water flows in a **cycle** – it's pumped up the hill by the wind, then it's released when it's needed.

Sofia: Yes, that's right. What's more, the system also provides our drinking water and water for use in agriculture.

Reporter: But where does the water come from?

Sofia: We use seawater.

Reporter: But you can't drink saltwater …

Sofia: We have a desalination plant to take the salt out of the seawater so it can be used in agriculture and as drinking water. We're constantly adding new water and taking stored water out of the cycle as we need to use it. In fact, I've just come from the desalination plant, where we're having some problems today. Something isn't working properly, and the replacement parts haven't arrived yet. We're a long way from the mainland, so delivery of anything takes at least a few days. If they don't come soon, we may have to ask people to use less water for a few days.

Reporter: You're a long way from everything out here, aren't you? It must be difficult sometimes.

Sofia: Well, it's a real challenge living here. On the other hand, we all love it. It can be a hard life, but I wouldn't live anywhere else.

🔊 **6.2**

Reporter: This is Andrew Thompson, reporting from the Spanish island of El Hierro, about 250 miles (400 kilometers) off the coast of Africa. It's pretty far from Madrid, which is nearly 1,250 miles (2,000 kilometers) away. Today, we're going to talk to two of the 11,000 people who live here, to find out what's so special about the island. First, this is Pedro Rodriguez, who owns a seafood restaurant on the island. Hello, Pedro.

Pedro: Hello, Andrew.

Reporter: So, how long have you lived on El Hierro?

Pedro: I haven't lived here for very long. I came from Madrid about five years ago.

Reporter: Don't you like it here?

Pedro: I love it here! I wish I had come a lot sooner than I did. I spent most of my life in Madrid.

Reporter: City life can be tough. I suppose island life is rather more relaxing.

Pedro: Exactly. El Hierro is my home now.

Reporter: So, what's so great about El Hierro?

Pedro: In the city, everyone hurries everywhere. You are surrounded by traffic, and you never feel like you can really relax. What's more, my career was in banking, which is an especially stressful job. I love the sound of the sea. I love the peace and quiet, and I feel free here. City life was never like that. When I was living in the city, I worked in banking, as I said. It paid well and I was able to buy my restaurant, but I should have left the city when I was a much younger man.

Reporter: So you love the quiet life on El Hierro, but is there anything else that makes El Hierro special?

Pedro: Well, for one thing, El Hierro is completely energy independent!

Reporter: Energy independent?

Pedro: Yes. In the past, the power on the island was provided by oil. A lot of money was paid to ship 40,000 barrels of oil over from the mainland every year. It cost the island over two million dollars a year. Now, all our energy is created right here on the island.

🔊 6.3

Reporter: And for more about that, we'll now talk to engineer Sofia Martinez.

Sofia: Hello, Andrew.

Reporter: I wonder if you could tell us about the way you generate energy here on El Hierro.

Sofia: Well, if you've spent a day or two here, you may have noticed we have a lot of wind.

Reporter: Yes. In fact, it's blowing pretty hard outside right now.

Sofia: Well, for about 3,000 hours, or for about 30% of the year, the wind here blows hard enough to turn wind turbines, which can provide electricity.

Reporter: Does El Hierro rely completely on wind to power the island?

Sofia: No. The island's wind turbines have a capacity of about 11 megawatts, about enough to power 3,500 homes, but it's only one element. The bigger problem is that the wind doesn't blow all the time, so the power source isn't consistent.

Reporter: So you need another energy source on windless days?

Sofia: That was the challenge: to create an energy generation system, or a network of systems, that could supply enough energy for the island all the time. And the solution was hydroelectric power.

Reporter: What is hydroelectric power exactly?

Sofia: Hydroelectric power is when energy is converted into another form, such as electricity. The initial source of this energy is from water.

Reporter: But doesn't hydroelectric power require a river and a dam? Isn't El Hierro too small for a river?

Sofia: A river with a dam is the usual way of producing hydroelectric power, but really, all you need is water that can move from a high place to a lower place to get energy from the water.

Reporter: OK …

Sofia: At the center of El Hierro is a dormant volcano – a volcano that is no longer active. In the middle of the volcano, we built a reservoir that holds over 17 million cubic feet (500,000 cubic meters) of water, at a height of 2,297 feet (700 meters) above sea level. So that's our water in a high place.

Reporter: But you don't get much rain here. What happens when all of the water runs out of the reservoir?

Sofia: Well, I mentioned the wind turbines. The wind power and the hydroelectric power are in a network together. When the wind is blowing, energy from the wind turbines pumps water up into the reservoir.

Reporter: So the wind turbines power the pumping station?

Sofia: Right. We also use the wind power for all of our electrical needs, when it blows. Then when the wind stops, we let water run out of the reservoir and through some turbines. The turbines turn generators and we have hydroelectric power we can access.

Reporter: So the water flows in a cycle – it's pumped up the hill by the wind, then it's released when it's needed.

Sofia: Yes, that's right. What's more, the system also provides our drinking water and water for use in agriculture.

Reporter: But where does the water come from?

Sofia: We use seawater.

Reporter: But you can't drink saltwater …

Sofia: We have a desalination plant to take the salt out of the seawater so it can be used in agriculture and as drinking water. We're constantly adding new water and taking stored water out of the cycle as we need to use it. In fact, I've just come from the desalination plant, where we're having some problems today. Something isn't working properly and the replacement parts haven't arrived yet. We're a long way from the mainland, so delivery of anything takes at least a few days. If they don't come soon, we may have to ask people to use less water for a few days.

Reporter: You're a long way from everything out here, aren't you? It must be difficult sometimes.

Sofia: Well, it's a real challenge living here. On the other hand, we all love it. It can be a hard life, but I wouldn't live anywhere else.

🔊 6.4

See script on page 132.

🔊 6.5

See script on page 132.

🔊 6.6

1 In certain states fracking is banned due to its dangerous effects on the environment.

2 Humans, animals, and the environment could all be threatened by the use of nuclear energy.

3 The community refuses to allow the power company to build a new plant by the river.

4 Salt is removed from the water at the desalination plant.

5 We are a completely energy-independent country.

6 I don't think we should use fossil fuels at all anymore.

🔊 6.7

Jane: As you all know, there's been a proposal that we should try to reduce our energy **consumption** here in the office, both to save money for the business and to help the environment. The **function** of this meeting today is to get your ideas on how to do this and hopefully to come up with a plan to take forward. Would anyone like to start? What are your views? Yes, Zara.

Zara: Well, if we really want to do something to save on electricity costs long-term, why don't we consider an alternative energy source? We could install some solar panels on the roof. That would generate plenty of environmentally friendly electricity.

Jane: That's not a bad idea. Would anyone like to add to Zara's comments? Allen?

Allen: It's true that we could go for a big solution like solar power generation. Even so, I think we could consider some rather simpler, smaller-scale ideas too, like changing to low-energy lightbulbs. There's a lot of potential to save energy there.

Jane: I think that's a great point, Allen. Abdul, would you like to expand on that?

Abdul: Yes. Allen's lightbulb idea is a really good one. Energy-efficient bulbs aren't hugely expensive to install. In addition, they pay for themselves quickly.

Jane: "Pay for themselves?"

Abdul: They don't use much energy, so they're cheap to run. It means they will soon save us more money than the cost of the new bulbs. Although these energy-efficient bulbs are expensive, we would save enough money in one year to pay for them.

Jane: I see. Do you have any other ideas?

Abdul: Yes. Some of the ideas are very simple: cleaning our dirty windows, for example. As a result of that, we'll allow more natural light in. Furthermore, we can turn off our computer screens when we get up from our desks.

Jane: Yes, Zara.

Zara: We could also consider turning off the air conditioning when it isn't too hot, so we can use less energy.

Jane: Great idea.

Zara: We could get rid of one of our photocopiers, too, as we don't really need two. The current machines use energy even when they're on standby.

Jane: Also a good plan. Now, I'd like to go back to Abdul. Abdul, you said we should consider smaller-scale solutions to our energy consumption here. Are you saying you're against installing a solar energy system?

Abdul: No, I really like that idea because once it's installed, the system will have a low operating cost, and it's an environmentally friendly way to generate electricity, which are two big positive points, but there are other considerations. For example, we'd have to look at the generating capacity of the system. It's very expensive to buy and install, and if it doesn't produce a lot of power, it'll end up costing rather than saving us money, at least for the first few years. The challenge is to choose ways of saving energy that also save money right now.

Allen: Yes, I agree with that. The other real environmental problem we have here in the office is trash. Most of us buy our lunch in plastic containers that have to be thrown away. It's a disgrace. We really should try to reduce the **volume** of trash we create here in the office.

Jane: Sorry, but that's not really what we're discussing right now. We can deal with waste and recycling later. Right now we're talking specifically about energy use.

Allen: Okay, fine. Sorry about that.

Zara: So, we were talking about turning off computer screens and turning off the air conditioning, but I don't think we should forget about installing solar panels, or a solar water heating system.

Jane: But there are some **drawbacks** to that, such as the installation cost, which Abdul mentioned.

Abdul: Right, and there's also the problem of ...

Simon: Can I just say, by the way ...

Jane: Sorry, but could you hold that thought until Abdul has finished, please?

Simon: Sure. Sorry.

Abdul: The fact is, both systems Zara mentioned are technically complex and expensive to install. There's also the problem of **maintenance**; we'd need to pay a technician to travel to make repairs if anything went wrong and for expensive parts that needed to be replaced. There could be a real decline in the amount of money we save if we ran into operational problems.

Jane: Can I just clarify something here? Abdul, is this **experimental** technology, or have alternative-energy generation systems been successful in other office environments?

Abdul: Well, every small-scale system is different because every building is different. The technology would have to be specially designed for our building in order to be **efficient**.

Allen: I can't help but feel that a solar energy project would be too ambitious. There would probably be technical **limitations** about the sort of system we could install on the office roof. I'm not sure it's even possible, or if the local government would let us.

Jane: I can assure you that the company wouldn't do anything unsafe or illegal.

Zara: It could be good publicity, though. We could market ourselves as a complete "green" business.

Simon: Maybe we should have some of our marketing people look at that. I think ...

Jane: We're getting sidetracked. Can we stick to the main points of the meeting? We should probably move on to the next part of the agenda, so I'd just like to summarize the key points so far. First of all, we want to immediately start making the simple energy-saving changes mentioned, such as cleaning the windows, turning off computer screens, and installing energy-saving lightbulbs. Second, we want to look into possible larger-scale alternative energy systems such as solar panels or a solar water-heating system. However, we need to do a lot of research in that area to see if we could get permission to install a system on the roof. A positive to installing a larger-scale project would be that it could generate good publicity for the company. Have I missed anything?

Abdul: You didn't mention ...

🔊 6.8

A: So, to summarize the key points so far: we agree that we want to reduce energy consumption and we want to consider an alternative energy source. Does anyone have anything to say about a solar energy system?

B: I'm more concerned about our water usage.

C: Sorry, but that's not really what we're discussing right now.

🔊 6.9

See script on page 142.

🔊 6.10

Professor: Good morning everyone. Today I'm going to talk about working in groups, both in education and in the workplace. I'll talk about why it's so important nowadays and we'll look at some ways to make sure that groups work successfully.

If you ask an employer, "what is the skill that you most look for in new employees?" they will often say it is the ability to work well with other people. That's because on the job, so much work is done in teams. Employees have to be able to collaborate to listen to other people's opinions, ask questions, respect differences, and resolve conflicts.

But not all working groups function well. There are a number of reasons for this. Sometimes the project is not defined clearly enough, so people don't really know what they have to do. Sometimes people feel that their opinions are not valued. Sometimes people complain that a majority of the work is done by a minority of the people.

OK, so there are several ways that groups can be helped to succeed. One thing is to make sure that the project has a clear timeline and that everyone in the group knows what has to be done by when. This helps keep everyone focused on the same goal.

Another way to help a group succeed is to divide up the work at the beginning of the project and to give everyone in the group a role – a specific job to do. Most groups assign roles according to what people are good at. For example, a person who is good at art might be the natural choice for designing a presentation or a logo.

There are different kinds of roles that people can have. Usually, you have a leader who also chairs the meetings. You should also have a recorder – someone who takes notes on what is discussed and agreed on in the meetings.

But a lot depends on the size of the group and the type of project. When you are planning your project, first work out your timeline. Then identify the different jobs that have to be done and make sure that everyone knows what their role is.

Now, I'd like to talk about …

UNIT 7

▶ Jen Lewin's Light and Sound Installations

Jen Lewin: Technology has been part of art since the beginning of art, whether it was, you know, the advent of charcoal to draw on a cave wall or paints. In this case, we're using, um, computers and computer systems and data and bits and bytes. But it's really, and from my perspective, it's no different than paint. I come into here, this is a new project, and it's really about combining the old and the new. It's going to be five different giant, um, lights, and they use aluminum frames and old Edison bulbs. And in the bulbs are small LEDs that we can project video into.

Lisa Tamiris Becker: Jen Lewin is an interactive new media artist. She does create computer mediated artworks that involve the viewer. She works with sound and light and encouraging the viewer to move around and activate parts of the artwork.

Jen Lewin: These are interactive platforms that are part of my pool sculpture, and they're meant to be jumped on and played on, and you step on them and they light up and project and send video messages to the other platforms, and you can create beautiful swirls of light and color.

Lisa Tamiris Becker: You know, what is art? What is technology? What is craft? That's an elusive question. I think if you go back to the most ancient roots of art, whether you go back to cave paintings, which existed in many different parts of the world, it was about the image that might have been represented, but it was also about the space and the light in which you were perceiving those images.

Jen Lewin: It's not surprising that this idea of interactive art with large groups of people is happening at a time when there's so much social media. We look at the Internet, suddenly there's all these examples of the Web being used to connect groups of people and to bring them together, and in my work I'm trying to do the same thing. I'm trying to bring 100 people together into a space to play with a sculpture in a much more networked and connected way.

Lisa Tamiris Becker: Art, architecture, and technologies of light, technologies of construction, etc. were combined to create total environments. So I think a lot of new media artists are returning to that idea.

🔊 7.1

Host: Hello from downtown. Overnight, the area's mystery graffiti artist has struck again. Although the **identity** of the painter remains unknown, their work is making an impact on the community. This large image has been painted on the side of an office building. A lot of people in the street on their way to work are stopping to look at it. Let's talk to a few of them and find out what they think of this latest spray-painted image.

Hello, excuse me?

Alex: Yes?

Host: I'm reporting on the recent increase in street art in the downtown area. Can I ask you a few questions?

Alex: Sure, no problem.

Host: What is your name?

Alex: My name is Alex.

Host: So, Alex, what do you think of this new artistic addition to the neighborhood?

Alex: This street art? I think it's great. It's something interesting to look at, and it looks good, doesn't it? I live around the corner, so this is on my doorstep.

Host: What do you like about it?

Alex: I just think it's cool – it has a distinctive style. At first glance, it looks like the painting was done in a few minutes. But in fact, it's not just spray painting; it's the work of a talented artist. It really decorates the area, and I think the **creativity** makes a very ugly neighborhood a lot better looking.

Host: Does everyone in the area like it?

Alex: Most of my neighbors do. We think this kind of thing could become a special feature of the area. It's a real shame that it's going to be covered up before many people have a chance to see it.

Host: Covered up?

Alex: The police are going to paint over it soon because street art is illegal.

Host: Oh, right. Yes, we'll come back to that in a minute. Thanks for talking to us.

Alex: No problem.

Host: Clearly some people really like the painting. However, there's also already been some **criticism** of the piece. Let's see what more we can find out about this side of the story.

Hello, excuse me?

Office worker: Yes?

Host: I'm finding out what people think of street art in this area. Can I ask you a few questions?

Office worker: I'm just on my way into the office, so you'll have to be quick.

Host: What do you think of this painting?

Office worker: I don't really like it. It's just graffiti, isn't it?

Host: What do you mean?

Office worker: The people who own this building didn't ask for this, did they? I mean, what **right** does this person have to spray paint their message here? If somebody wants to express themselves in this way, they should get permission. I'd be really angry if someone did this in my neighborhood.

Host: Do you think it's a work of art?

Office worker: No, not at all. Art is an exhibition in an art museum. This is just somebody spraying paint onto a wall in the middle of the night. Like I said, it's just **self-expression**.

Host: Yes, I see what you mean. Thanks for taking a minute to talk.

Office worker: No problem.

Host: I think it would be a good idea to get a professional view on this now. I have a local police officer with me.

Hello, and thanks for talking with me today.

Police officer: Hi, no problem.

Host: What's your view on the latest work of the mystery painter?

Police officer: Well, to be honest, as a piece of art, I actually really like it, despite the fact that it's illegal. However, I also completely agree with the person you just spoke with. We can't have this sort of thing. It *is* vandalism, and it *is* against the law.

Host: It's against the law?

Police officer: Yes. Vandalism is a crime because it is intentionally damaging property that belongs to the city or to other people.

Host: I'm very interested to hear you call this piece of vandalism a work of *art*.

Police officer: It is artistic, though, isn't it? I couldn't paint that. The person who did this, especially very quickly and at night, is very creative. This painting is really expressive, but I have to stress that it's illegal, and therefore we're going to paint over it later today. We **remove** all graffiti because it's the law.

Host: What would you recommend for people who want to express themselves through street art?

Police officer: My recommendation? Well, if this artist wants to paint where everyone can see the artwork, he or she should get permission. We can work with street artists to create art that people have chosen to have in their community.

Host: So you mean you can give someone permission to paint graffiti?

Police officer: Yes, well, sort of. However, they have to apply for a permit and get approval and so on. This makes it a legal activity rather than vandalism.

Host: Thanks a lot for talking with us.

Police officer: My pleasure.

Host: Next, I have an art critic here who agrees with some people about the quality of the latest street painting. This is Simone James, an art gallery owner and art critic. Hello, Simone.

Simone: Hello.

Host: Simone, could you **comment** on the latest creation of our illegal painter?

Simone: Many people think that the painting is just rough spray painting. However, the fact of the matter is the artist has created a very expressive piece of artwork using very basic tools and materials. The color scheme and the **composition** work very well together. It's a strong piece. If this artist were to exhibit and sell their work, I think he or she could make a lot of money.

Host: Do you have any idea who the artist might be?

Simone: I have no idea at all, but technically, the work really is very good, so I'd like to find out!

Host: Thank you very much. Finally, there's one more person I'd like to speak with. This is Joseph, who's 13. Joseph, what do you think of the mystery artist's latest painting?

Joseph: I wish I'd done it! I think it's really good.

Host: What do you like about it?

Joseph: I think this type of art is a really good way of expressing your ideas. I don't know who did it, but I guess it's a young person like me and by doing this kind of art in this way, on the streets, the artist is communicating a message about how young people feel.

Host: OK, thanks Joseph. So we've had a full range of responses to the latest street art in the downtown area. However, the true identity of the graffiti painter remains a mystery.

See script on page 153.

Robert: ... Okay everyone, are we ready to get back to business? The next item to look at today is the proposed budget to continue paying for public art in City Park. We've recently had to spend a lot of money repairing and restoring the sculpture we commissioned last year because vandals have broken parts of it. We've also spent a lot of time and money removing graffiti from it. The city accounting office has confirmed that the total bill for cleaning and repairs has come to more than $7,000 this year. There's been a proposal that we sell the sculpture, stop paying for new public art, and use the money to pay for a new recreation center. Would anyone like to comment on this?

Lisa: Yes, Robert, I'd like to say something.

Robert: OK, Lisa. Go ahead.

Lisa: Personally, I'm not really sure that paying for art is an appropriate way to spend public money. We assume that we should invest in art since so many other parks have art, but in reality, it's costing us a lot of money, and the art doesn't really benefit the city's population. A lot of people simply don't **appreciate** or like to **interpret** art. The truth of the matter is, more people would use and benefit from a recreation center.

Robert: If I understand you correctly, Lisa, you're saying that we shouldn't spend more money commissioning art?

Lisa: Well, yes. I think public art is a waste of money.

Robert: I see. Yes, Ahmad, would you like to add something?

Ahmad: Yes, thank you Robert. I see what you mean, Lisa, and I'm not an expert, but it's been said that art, and appreciating art, is an important part of any culture. OK, it's true that some people say we're wasting money by commissioning art, but the fact of matter is that art is an important part of any culture. Art can help make us proud of our city, and a lot of people really enjoy looking at it. We had 400,000 visitors to our art museum last year, so people are interested in art.

Marco: That's true, Ahmad. Research has demonstrated over and over again that art can have a very positive effect on people.

Robert: Thank you Ahmad and Marco. Yes, Pei, did you want to add something?

Pei: Ahmad and Marco have good points, but one other thing to remember is that although many people think that art is worth a lot of money because it's by famous artists or because the city invested in it, we don't actually know that the art is worth anything. Look at the sculpture there now, for example. Since it's been damaged and repaired so much, we don't know if we can sell the sculpture, even to a private collector. Do we really want to invest in more art?

Robert: OK, thank you all for your comments. I think we need to find out how much new art would cost us. We'll have to get an art expert to **analyze** the pieces we like and maybe we can **restore** them rather than buy new ones.
Would anyone else like to make a comment? Yes, Marco?

Marco: If we decide against commissioning the public art, we'll need to put something in its place.

Lisa: Like building the recreation center instead.

Pei: You say that, Lisa, but I am not sure that would be popular enough. We'd need to talk to a lot of people to gather data and opinions about whether they like the art or if they want a new building, but this might **reveal** some really good ideas we haven't thought of.

Robert: Yes, I think you're right, Pei. Let's put together a survey. This will include commissioning more art and building the recreation center. Also, we can include three or four other ideas. Then we can get people to look at it. Is there anything else anyone would like to say? Yes, Claudia?

Claudia: For me, there's a public safety issue here. The police reports have shown that kids climb on the public art we have there now. This happens almost every night, and they're breaking it and writing graffiti on it. This artwork really is causing more problems than it's worth.

Ahmad: You may be right, Claudia, but I wonder if it's the location of the artwork rather than the artwork itself that's the problem.

Lisa: In other words, Ahmad, you think we should move it?

Ahmad: I think moving it might solve the vandalism problem. It seems as if the art is just costing us money for cleaning and repairs. If we were to **display** it in a different spot, we probably wouldn't have these problems. Plus, we'd still contribute to the culture of the city by having the art available.

Pei: I agree with Ahmad. I think we could consider moving the sculpture to the front of city hall, next to the hospital, or possibly even inside the main shopping mall. In fact, the shopping mall has already expressed interest in this because they believe artwork could be a tourist attraction. If we planned it properly, we could get people to see the artwork and do some shopping at the same time!

Lisa: So, Pei, what you're saying is that you'd definitely rather keep commissioning art but just put it in other locations?

Pei: Yes, that's right.

Robert: OK, yes, those ideas make sense. I think we need to do more research here. First, we need to **focus on** identifying some places that the art could be displayed. We need to **reject** any places where we feel vandals would be likely to damage it. Second, we need to consider the cost of the current art, the sculpture that is already there.

Pei: There's one other point I'd like to raise.

Robert: OK. Go ahead, Pei.

Pei: What would we do with the money if we didn't commission any new art and didn't build the recreation center?

Robert: You ask a good question. The money would be put back into the budget, and we'd have to determine a project that reflects what people really want.

Ahmad: Well, a recreation center or any other center is a good thing, but it isn't art. I think our children need to see art in public places, especially the work of a famous artist, right here in our city. We need to have a balance of investment in leisure activities and public art in the lives of our children.

Robert: OK, I think we need to look into this. We need to explore our options in more detail.

Are there any other comments on this topic? No? OK. We'll move on, then …

🔊 **7.4**

See script on page 164.

🔊 **7.5**

Anchor: Good morning! In today's program, we're looking at an important decision for every undergraduate, and that's how to choose your major. Here to give us some advice is Anita Rao, a career advisor from City University. Welcome to the show.

Anita Rao: Thank you.

Anchor: First of all, I'd like to ask: what advice do you give to students who really can't decide on a major?

Anita Rao: I think the most important thing is to choose something you like. Identify the subjects that

you are most interested in and the classes that you have enjoyed most.

Anchor: That seems logical.

Anita Rao: Yes. But many students forget that. A lot of students nowadays are so concerned about employment prospects after they graduate!

Anchor: Isn't it a good idea to think about making money?

Anita Rao: I think it's certainly good to think about how you might make a living. But you have to be realistic. A lot of students say, "I want to study computer science because I'll make a lot of money." But do you have the math skills? Computer science involves a lot of math ability. It can be difficult and frustrating. Yes, there are many good jobs out there, but not everybody has the ability to be a computer programmer.

Anchor: Is it a good idea to get some experience in the field?

Anita Rao: Absolutely. I encourage students to look for summer jobs or internships. That way they get a sense of what the working world is really like. Often they come back in the fall with a much more realistic idea of what they would like to do.

Anchor: What other advice do you have for students?

Anita Rao: Don't worry too much. Unless you are studying in a professional area, such as medicine, your major will not usually limit you to a specific career.

Anchor: Really?

Anita Rao: Yes. Many people don't find work in their major field, and most people change careers several times. What is important to employers are the general skills that you get in college: the ability to speak and write clearly, to research information, and to work with other people.

UNIT 8

▶ **Baby Boomers' Retirement Style**

Ben Tracy (reporter): This is retirement, boomer style.

Gordon Feld: This is what retirement should be.

Ben Tracy: Gordon Feld and his equally adventurous wife Peggy spend their days zipping through the Arizona desert.

So this is retirement? Where is the shuffleboard?

Gordon Feld: Nah, that's for old people.

Ben Tracy: They bought a home in this retirement community 45 miles from Phoenix. Developments like this cater to boomers concerned about cost and lifestyle. The average house sells for about $200,000, and $100 a month buys the amenities many boomers demand.

Woman: They're highly educated, they have high expectations, um, of what they want in their life, and they expect to live a long time.

Man 1: Helmets on.

Ben Tracy: In fact, 86% of boomers say they'll be more active in retirement than their parents were. But to pay for it, 70% will keep working at least part time, and 42% are delaying full-time retirement because of hits to their retirement accounts and home values during the recession.

Man 2: They're having to work longer trying to rebuild their investment portfolio and their 401(k)s.

Ben Tracy: 62-year-old Jerry Axton is still running his handmade furniture business, even though he's been living in this retirement village for two years.

Jerry Axton: Doing nothing doesn't sound very exciting, and retirement borderlines to me doing nothing.

Ben Tracy: Most of these boomers feel their sunset years are still a ways down the road. Ben Tracy, CBS News, Buckeye, Arizona.

🔊 8.1

Host: Hello and welcome to the *Money and Finance* podcast. I'm your host, Ian Brown, and today's topic is **retirement**. In the past, giving up work in their sixties signaled the end of an active, exciting life for people. It was seen as a time for staying at home, doing the gardening, and being very careful with money. Twenty years ago, most people planned to leave a large sum of money to their children upon their death and didn't spend a lot on themselves once they started to rely on their retirement funds, whether those came from an employee **pension** plan or Social Security.

But times have changed. People nowadays don't think of the sixties as old. People who have exercised and eaten a good diet throughout their lives have plenty of energy to enjoy life, no matter what age they retire at. Many of today's older people see retirement as a reward for a lifetime of hard work, and rather than saving their money to give to their children, they're spending it – on luxuries, travel, new cars, and meals out, and because they worked hard and saved hard for their retirement, they have plenty of money to spend. As a group, the over-60s in the United States have over 25 trillion dollars in **assets**: **property**, money in the bank, investments, and so on. Retirement assets accounted for 36% of the household financial assets

in the United States. The average married person between the ages of 65 and 74 spent 26% of the household income on food and entertainment. Rick and Nadia Jones are typical of this new approach to retirement. I asked them to share their thoughts.

Nadia: Well, in my working life I was a banker and Rick was in business. We both retired at 65, and since that time, we've traveled a lot and have had years of excitement and fun. A lot of our friends are doing the same. We're still healthy and we love traveling, so why shouldn't we? I had to persuade Rick to agree to the idea at first. It just wasn't like that for our parents. However, we've managed to save enough money to **permit** us to live the life we've always wanted, and I think we've earned it.

Rick: We've been to Alaska and Europe – and Nadia loves the weather in the Caribbean! We've been there three times.

Host: According to one survey, 20 years ago, most of today's older people believed they would work in the garden, read, and babysit their grandchildren. However, retired people now want to do more exciting things! Do you agree with this?

Nadia: I do, I think. We worked hard during our careers to **ensure** that our two daughters had a good education. They're both married and working now. I want to be involved in my children's lives, but I do also want adventure! We live close to both our daughters and offer to babysit our grandchildren regularly, but we're not a free day care!

Rick: Exactly. We don't have any **dependents** anymore. Our daughters need to work hard and save their money just as we've done. Our savings allow us to live the life we've always wanted. This is our chance to have some fun, and we don't want to stay home all day gardening and watching television. Our daughters have agreed to support our choices, and we hope they'll make the same choices for themselves one day.

Nadia: I think our parents' **generation** thought it was really important to save for the next generation, to give money to their children, but our generation doesn't think that way.

Rick: We've talked to our daughters about it. They understand that the money is ours to spend. They also understand that as long as we're in shape and healthy, we might as well enjoy life. Our home is also worth about $272,000. We are not planning on selling it, so they'll get that eventually.

Host: Recent research shows that about two-thirds of older people agree with Rick and Nadia and plan to leave their home to their children, and no money. But what about the next generation? Today's working generation is probably facing a more difficult retirement than their parents. Pensions are getting smaller, many companies are no longer providing pensions at all, and the average age of retirement is increasing. According to the U.S. Census Bureau, about 16% of Americans aged 65 and over are still working, but that number is increasing. Should these parents be doing more? Rick?

Rick: I think we both feel we've done our part as parents. We have many happy, healthy years ahead of us and still have other things we want to do with our lives, and now we're doing them. I'd advise everyone else to do the same.

🔊 8.2

See script on page 175.

🔊 8.3

Mika: Hello. My name is Mika. I'm going to discuss how things are changing for elderly people in Japan. I'll begin by explaining the importance of family in Japan and present some figures that explain how the population is changing. Finally, I'll talk about the way the Japanese government is dealing with the aging population.

Family in Japan has been very important since the days of my **ancestors**. However, while the extended family is very important in other countries, the focus in Japan is on the bond among children, parents, grandparents, and so on. Of course, this means that in many cases, when elderly people can no longer take care of themselves, they move in with their children.

Japan has one of the highest life expectancies in the world. Its population is about 127 million. If you look at the data I've provided, you will note that it **indicates** there were about 33 million people in 2014 over the age of 65 in Japan, nearly 26% of the population. By 2050, Japan's population will be about 99 million, and 35% of the population will be over 65. The population of children under the age of 14 is expected to fall from about 19 million to about 18 million in 2020 and 12 million by 2050. This can be traced back to a low fertility rate, that is, the number of children being born to a woman during the time she is able to have children. That fertility rate has dropped to just below 1.5 children per woman. Young Japanese people are waiting longer than their parents' generation to get married, and when they do, they're

having fewer children. Young people now enjoy a lot of free time in their twenties and thirties, but this also results in the same issues that other countries are facing: more and more elderly people to take care of, with fewer younger people to be **providers**. Since the population of Japan is set to decrease by 22% by 2050, this means a loss of about 28 million residents.

The Japanese government has taken steps to deal with the situation. Most Japanese people between the ages of 40 and 65 pay an income tax that goes to help those over 65. The over-65s don't get the money directly, but the government supports them. Even elderly people living at home with family have a care worker who makes sure they have everything they need. Some elderly people go to a day-care center a few times a week, where they can share meals and **participate** in social activities. Those elderly people who don't live with family generally live in **institutions**, with about nine people living in one home. Each has a bedroom, and they share a living room and kitchen. This enables them to have some independence and to feel cared for at the same time.

Ahmet: My name is Ahmet. Thank you Mika for your interesting presentation. My topic today is how elderly people are cared for in Turkey. First, I'll give some background on how the elderly are usually cared for. After that, I'll talk about some of the drawbacks and benefits of this system, and I'll finish by explaining the challenges ahead.

Mika explained that it is becoming more and more common in Japan for elderly people to live in institutions when their ability to care for themselves declines. Moving old people into nursing homes allows the younger generation to continue their lives without having to worry about daily care for an aging parent. However, in Turkey, 80% of households have an older person in them. Many families see this as the natural solution to dealing with old age. As parents, we **devote** ourselves to our children. In turn, as adults, we devote ourselves to our aging parents. Most people my age have a grandparent living at home.

The system has drawbacks, both for the families caring for elderly people and for the elderly people themselves. Those responsible for the welfare of an elderly person can feel that they aren't free to do as they like in their own home. The older people being cared for may also not feel completely free and dislike the way things are done by their caregivers. Living closely together in forced circumstances can raise tensions. However, there are many benefits to these arrangements. In many households, older people **contribute** to the family by participating in domestic jobs and helping with childcare. This gives them something to do and a sense of **responsibility**.

Turkey's population is just over 80 million today. If you look at the graph I've provided, you will see that more than 5 million people, or around 6%, are over 65. For now, the solution is for Turks to continue caring for the elderly at home.

🔊 8.4

See script on page 186.

🔊 8.5

Presenter: Welcome to the College Career Center! Here you will find resources for everything to do with finding a job or planning a career. We encourage you to visit us early and often, and to keep your long-term goals in mind as you progress through college.

Most students come to us first for information about jobs. We have job listings for part-time jobs on and off campus, which can be a good way to make some extra cash on the weekends. We can also help you find internships. Some internships are unpaid, but an internship with a good company can be a great experience and lead to a paid position later.

We offer workshops to help you prepare your résumé so that it shows you in your best light. As a student, you may not have a lot of work experience, but if you have done some community service or held a leadership position, that all goes into your résumé. Also, don't forget your online identity! Many employers look at your profile on social media before they decide to call you for an interview. We can help you create a good online identity.

Every spring, the career center organizes job fairs, when companies come to campus to meet with students. This is a good way to network with companies that you are interested in. You can also ask questions about the company and find out about future opportunities.

Maybe you'd like to go to graduate or professional school. Here you can research the different programs that are available and find out about financial aid for further study.

So, there are a lot of great resources here at the career center. My name is Scott, and I'd be happy to answer any questions that you have.

CREDITS

The authors and publishers acknowledge the following sources of copyright material and are grateful for the permissions granted. While every effort has been made, it has not always been possible to identify the sources of all the material used, or to trace all copyright holders. If any omissions are brought to our notice, we will be happy to include the appropriate acknowledgements on reprinting and in the next update to the digital edition, as applicable.

Text credits

Map on p. 63 adapted from "Influenza Pandemic Risk Index – Risk of Spread 2012". Copyright © Verisk Maplecroft. Reproduced with kind permission; Text on pp. 154–155 adapted from "10 Things You Must See in the Louvre" by Daisy de Plume, of THATMuse (Treasure Hunt at the Museum), Bonjour Paris website. Copyright © 2015 France Media Ltd. Reproduced with kind permission.

Photo credits

Key: C = Center, L = Left, R = Right.

p. 12: Cultura RM Exclusive/Peter Muller/Getty Images; pp. 14–15: Nic Cleave Photography/Alamy; p. 20, p. 157: Bloomberg/Getty Images; p. 24: PeopleImages.com/DigitalVision/Getty Images; p. 32: Inti St Clair/Blend Images/Getty Images; p. 34: Jose A. Bernat Bacete/Moment/Getty Images; pp. 36–37: wunkley/Alamy; p. 41: Peter Cade/Iconica/Getty Images; p. 45: Caiaimage/Sam Edwards/Getty Images; p. 46: andylewisphoto/iStock/Getty Images; p. 50: Ariel Skelley/Blend Images/Getty Images; pp. 58–59: Boston Globe/Getty Images; p. 70: Design Pics/Getty Images; p. 72 (L): Blend Images/Shutterstock; p. 72 (R): Tetra Images/Getty Images; p. 75 (L): Monkey Business Images Ltd/Getty Images; p. 75 (R): Rubberball/Mike Kemp/Getty Images; pp. 80–81: Minden Pictures/Getty Images; p. 84: Al Seib/Los Angeles Times/Getty Images; p. 87: STR/AFP/Getty Images; p. 90: CBS Photo Archive/CBS/Getty Images; p. 96 (L): NASA/Getty Images News/Getty Images; p. 96 (C): Hiroya Minakuchi/Minden Pictures/Getty Images; p. 96 (R): Eco/Universal Images Group/Getty Images; pp. 102–103: Donald Nausbaum/Photographer's Choice/Getty Images; p. 111: Vladitto/iStock/Getty Images; p. 122 (L): Wavebreakmedia Ltd/Getty Images Plus/Getty Images; p. 122 (C): John Fedele/Blend Images/Getty Images; p. 122 (R): Hero Images/Getty Images; pp. 124–125: Paul Souders/Photonica World/Getty Images; p. 129: Ian Aitken/AWL Images/Getty Images; p. 136: Spaces Images/Blend Images/Getty Images; p. 144: Geber86/Vetta/Getty Images; pp. 146–147: Brian Kersey/Getty Images News/Getty Images; p. 151: Jeff Spielman/Photographer's Choice; p. 166: pepifoto/iStock/Getty Images; pp. 168–169: Chung Sung-Jun/Getty Images News/Getty Images; p. 173: J.D. Pooley/Getty Images News/Getty Images; p. 179: Asanka Brendon Ratnayake/Lonely Planet Images/Getty Images.

Front cover photographs by (woman) IZO/Shutterstock and (street) f11photo/Shutterstock.

Illustrations

by Oxford Designers & Illustration: p. 114.

Video Stills Supplied by BBC Worldwide Learning.

Video Supplied by BBC Worldwide Learning.

Corpus

Development of this publication has made use of the Cambridge English Corpus (CEC). The CEC is a multi-billion word computer database of contemporary spoken and written English. It includes British English, American English, and other varieties of English. It also includes the Cambridge Learner Corpus, developed in collaboration with the University of Cambridge ESOL Examinations. Cambridge University Press has built up the CEC to provide evidence about language use that helps to produce better language teaching materials

Cambridge Dictionaries

Cambridge dictionaries are the world's most widely used dictionaries for learners of English. The dictionaries are available in print and online at dictionary.cambridge.org. Copyright © Cambridge University Press, reproduced with permission.

Typeset by emc design ltd

Audio production by CityVox New York

INFORMED BY TEACHERS

Classroom teachers shaped everything about *Prism*. The topics. The exercises. The critical thinking skills. The On Campus sections. Everything. We are confident that *Prism* will help your students succeed in college because teachers just like you helped guide the creation of this series.

Prism Advisory Panel

The members of the *Prism* Advisory Panel provided inspiration, ideas, and feedback on many aspects of the series. *Prism* is stronger because of their contributions.

Gloria Munson
University of Texas, Arlington

Kim Oliver
Austin Community College

Gregory Wayne
Portland State University

Julaine Rosner
Mission College

Dinorah Sapp
University of Mississippi

Christine Hagan
George Brown College/Seneca College

Heidi Lieb
Bergen Community College

Stephanie Kasuboski
Cuyahoga Community College

Global Input

Teachers from more than 500 institutions all over the world provided valuable input through:
- Surveys
- Focus Groups
- Reviews